TEN ONE-ACT PLAYS
FOR WOMEN

SELECTED BY

ELIZABETH EVERARD

Director of the International One-act Play Theatre

Editor of
"THREE PRIZE ONE-ACT PLAYS AND TWO OTHERS"
"TWELVE ONE-ACT PLAYS"
"THREE PRIZE ONE-ACT PLAYS 1934–1935"

GEORGE G. HARRAP & CO. LTD.
LONDON TORONTO BOMBAY SYDNEY

First published 1944
by GEORGE G. HARRAP & CO. LTD.
182 *High Holborn, London, W.C.1*

Copyright.   All rights reserved

BOOK
PRODUCTION
WAR ECONOMY
STANDARD

MADE IN GREAT BRITAIN.   PRINTED BY J. AND J. GRAY, EDINBURGH

PREFACE

THERE is at present much talk of a rebirth of the theatre. That this is not just another case of wishful thinking is, perhaps, proved by the activities of such bodies as the *Council for the Encouragement of Music and the Arts*. Yet one feels that, unless an enthusiasm is shown and a demand definitely voiced for the one-act play, the professional theatre will continue its neglect of this most vital and vivid form of dramatic art. (A notable exception, Mr Denis Eadie, alone of London managers, consistently produced this type of play up to the time of his retirement.)

This neglect on the part of the professional theatre is the more inexplicable when one considers that this form of drama has possibilities no less great than any other form of artistic effort. Its economy alone excludes mere padding—a fault by no means absent from the longer type of play. It calls for a crisp, incisive simplicity, a quick march to its crisis, and a swift, logical summing-up at the climax.

Fortunately for dramatic art, the unaccountable attitude towards the one-act play shown by the professional theatre is not shared by the amateur stage. It is, indeed, due to the certainty of the support of the amateur player that a collection such as this is made possible. All honour, then, to the amateur players who, despite the many inescapable difficulties of war-time—depleted ranks, fewer meeting-places—are still producing plays up and down the country.

This selection has been made for the women who are overcoming these difficulties: Women's Institutes and Towns-women's Guilds, Girls' Clubs, dramatic societies of the Y.W.C.A., and similar organizations.

It has been said that plays for women are often written

down to a low standard. That cannot, I think, be charged against the ten plays which comprise the present volume. The work of such experienced playwrights as T. B. Morris and Vincent Godefroy would alone refute any such charge. All ten have undergone the acid test of production, whilst four of them are prize-winners.

While the plays will be produced mainly by amateurs, they are, I submit, well worth the attention of the professional player. Whatever economic excuses may be pleaded for their neglect by theatrical managers in London and elsewhere, those theatres which enjoy State support are less circumscribed.

It can scarcely be the considered policy of the C.E.M.A., for example, that all forms of dramatic art save one are worthy of its support. Music, opera, ballet, and full-length plays of every sort but no one-act play of any description—would be an incredible attitude to adopt. Is it too much, then, to hope that the one-act play also will be given an honoured place in those theatres which enjoy the support of the *Council for the Encouragement of Music and the Arts?*

ELIZABETH EVERARD

The International One-act Play Theatre
   60 Earlsfield Road, London, S.W.18

NOTE

All performing rights reserved.

CONTENTS

APPLE-PIE ORDER

A COSTUME COMEDY

by T. B. Morris

CHARACTERS

HORTENSE-MARIE, *the first Duchess, lady-in-waiting*
HARRIET-THEODOSIE, *the second Duchess, lady-in-waiting*
BASTIAN, *a page*
YSABEAU ⎫
JEHANNE ⎬ *maids of honour*
MELISANDE ⎭
CLEMENCE-OLYMPE-HIPPEASTRA, *Queen of Bon-Rebours*
ALYS, *a kitchen-wench*

SCENE: A room in the Royal Palace at Rave, capital of the small and probably unheard-of kingdom of Bon-Rebours, at almost any time in the Age of Chivalry or thereabout.

SCENE I: *A summer afternoon*
SCENE II: *The following day*
SCENE III: *A month later*

APPLE-PIE ORDER

THE SETTING: *A throne-like chair, somewhere upstage, preferably on a dais, a bench downstage L., and a stool or two are all the essential furniture. Additions to the scene may be made as desired, including coloured shields on the walls and a gay coat-of-arms on a shield above the chair. The setting may be simple curtains or plain walls hung with something to imitate tapestries. An unglazed window upstage, giving a view of medieval gardens (see contemporary paintings) will greatly help, but the window may be represented by a gap in the curtains upstage L. if desired. Entrances C. L., and upstage R.*

Setting and costumes should be as beautiful as possible. The latter may really be of any period from XIth to XVth century, or 'fairy-tale.'

SCENE I: A SUMMER AFTERNOON

Music. Either something sweet to fit the period or something eccentric such as a 'jazzed' version of Summer is icumen in. *The curtain rises to discover Hortense and Harriet sitting on the bench, asleep. They are back to back, Hortense sitting at one end with her feet on the floor, Harriet taking up nearly the whole length of the bench, her feet up on it, and using Hortense as a back-rest. Hortense's hands are primly folded across her stomach, to which she clutches a ball of silk. Harriet's hands are stuck up stiffly from the elbows, still holding the skein of silk from which the ball was being wound. They are snoring alternately in different styles, and their upper parts are moving rhythmically backward and forward as each pushes the other. They are middle-aged, dressed in rich dark materials to contrast with the maids of honour, and with impressive head-dresses. In appearance they*

8

*may be a pair or else as violently contrasted as possible, but
Hortense tries to be prim and dignified, while Harriet is not
without roguishness and juicy chuckles. After a moment of this
the music stops, and Ysabeau, a pretty young girl, peeps on R.,
amused. She laughs quietly, then beckons to Bastian, a young
and mischievous page, who looks over her shoulder.*

BASTIAN. *Cochon d'or!* They're at it again, the silly old
trouts! Look at them, Lady Ysabeau. One day the Queen
will catch them, and they'll have very small beer for at least
a fortnight.

YSABEAU. I wonder whether the Duchess Harriet-Theodosie
will ever manage to push the Duchess Hortense-Marie right
off that bench?

BASTIAN. She certainly tries hard enough, but Hortense is a
good resister.

YSABEAU. I should hate to sleep with Harriet. She must
want nearly all the bed.

BASTIAN. I should hate to sleep with either of them.

YSABEAU [*hastily*]. Well, we won't go into that. [*Chuckling*]
But what are we going to do about them this time?

BASTIAN. We can't use a wet sponge again. Suppose I tip
up the bench [*indicating Harriet*] at her end. That'll topple one
over t'other.

YSABEAU [*laughing*]. No. You might hurt the old dears,
and we don't want to do that. Besides, they'd see us. I
know . . .

[*She pulls out the long feather that Bastian wears in his cap
and tiptoes across the stage.*

BASTIAN. Here! I say . . .

[*But appreciation of the joke overcomes his irritation, and
he chuckles as he watches Ysabeau tickle first one nose and
then the other. This goes on for a little while, Harriet and
Hortense making funny faces and movements in their sleep;
then, with final snores, they wake with starts, Harriet slipping*

flat on the bench and pushing Hortense off the end of it.
Harriet still holds the silk. Ysabeau and Bastian run off
L. and R. laughing quietly, before they are seen.

HORTENSE. What is it?

HARRIET. Where am I?

HORTENSE. ⎫ You've been asleep again. [*Pause, then indig-*
HARRIET. ⎭ *nantly*] I haven't.

> [*They scramble up awkwardly.*

HORTENSE. You were lying down on the bench.

HARRIET. Well, you were on the floor.

HORTENSE. ⎫ If that isn't being asleep, I don't know what is.
HARRIET. ⎭

HORTENSE. You pushed me off the seat. And, my dear, you really must—it's a delicate matter to mention, but—you must do something about your snoring. I mean, as second lady-in-waiting to Queen Clemence-Olympe-Hippeastra you should——

HARRIET. I'm not second lady-in-waiting to Queen Clemence-Olympe-Hippeastra. I'm first lady-in-waiting to——

HORTENSE. No, you're not. I am.

HARRIET. Oh, my dear! What an entirely mistaken impression——

HORTENSE. My dear *Duchess*——

HARRIET. My *dear* Duchess——

HORTENSE. —you are utterly in error.

HARRIET. —you snore just as much as I do—that is, as much as you say I do—only worse.

> [*By this time Hortense has walked round and round Harriet,*
> *tangling her in her silk.*]

My good woman—what do you think you are? A spider?

HORTENSE [*confused*]. There, there! Your fault entirely. You will get involved in things. Now sit still and leave everything to me.

> [*Hortense continues in the wrong direction.*

HARRIET. No, no, idiot! The other way about.

HORTENSE. You mustn't call a duchess an idiot.

HARRIET. A duchess may call another duchess almost any-thing—[*chuckling*] especially if it happens to be true.

HORTENSE [*primly*]. Thank you for the permission, darling. I shall certainly avail myself of it.

[*By this time Harriet has been disentangled, and the two sit and continue the silk winding, in frigid silence. But Harriet has some news which she is bursting to tell, so the silence doesn't last long. After a few covert glances at Hortense she plunges.*]

HARRIET. Have you heard the latest?

HORTENSE. Latest what?

HARRIET. News, of course. What do you think?

HORTENSE [*loftily*]. I never think—er—I mean I never retail scandal, as you know, Harriet-Theodosie.

HARRIET. No, indeed, Hortense-Marie. Your trade is rather more of the *wholesale* order, isn't it? Anyway, I was only asking you to listen——

HORTENSE [*indifferently*]. Am I interested, do you think? [*Pause; then curiosity overcomes her. She adds eagerly*] What is it?

HARRIET. The King is at it again.

HORTENSE. At it again? [*Primly*] That sounds dreadfully vulgar, and we ladies-in-waiting cannot be too careful not to descend into vulgarity. [*Eagerly*] Do you mean he's started another *affair*?

HARRIET. He has.

HORTENSE. Oh dear, dear! The poor Queen!

HARRIET. She's used to it by now. This will be the . . . [*counts rapidly on her fingers, her lips moving*] . . . the forty-seventh.

HORTENSE. How very wrong of his Grace. [*Primly*] Well, we mustn't discuss it. [*Reproachfully*] My dear, how can you? Fancy counting them! [*Calmly*] As a matter of fact, it will be the forty-eighth.

HARRIET [*twinkling*]. There! [*Pause.*

HORTENSE [*inquisitively*]. Who is she?

HARRIET [*her head closer, to enjoy a good gossip*]. That little new maid of honour, Jehanne.

HORTENSE. The latest maid of honour is—er—usual with the King. But surely this one is the won't-melt-butter kind? Only the day before yesterday I was thinking how nice it was to have *one* maid of honour about the place who could really be called a—you know what I mean? I thought she was demure and shy.

HARRIET. Other people's shyness doesn't make much difference to the King. Rolls off him exactly like—like water off a cow's back.

HORTENSE. Duck's back, dear. Duck's back.

HARRIET. Anyway, she is shy, still. The King hasn't progressed beyond the merest flirtation—yet. But you know how it is—the woman runs away, the man pursues.

HORTENSE. Not at all. It was quite the other way about with my duke. H'm, h'm! I mean—er—there, I don't know what I did mean, now. The worst of you, Harriet-Theodosie, is that you will prattle on so.

HARRIET. I wonder what Lady Melisande will have to say about it.

HORTENSE. Lady Melisande—pah! I'd like to have had the spanking of her when she was little.

HARRIET. Much as I object to *agreeing* with you, my dear, I must say that I think it's about time she was put in her place. For the past six weeks—a long time for one of the King's affairs to last—she's been giving herself so many airs that there have been draughts all over the palace.

HORTENSE. Scandalous! If it weren't for the food and the feather-beds, I'd have retired from Court long ago.

HARRIET. I always think it such a pity that kings have to marry royalty, and female royalty is so often—er——

HORTENSE. I'd rather have the dear Queen, whatever her

looks, than these stuck-up young fly-by-nights of maids of honour.

HARRIET [*chuckling*]. Yes. But then, you're not the King, are you, dear?

[*Jehanne, a lovely young girl, shy and unsophisticated, enters, R.*]

Oh, Jehanne! We were just wondering—er, yes—*wondering* about you, child.

[*Jehanne, being nicely brought up, drops a respectful curtsy.*] There, there, my dear. Don't bother to curtsy to us.

HORTENSE. Speak for yourself, Harriet-Theodosie.

HARRIET. You see, we're not accustomed here to—er—respect from our youngers. Not that I think it necessary, in these modern days.

HORTENSE. I think it very necessary.

JEHANNE [*shyly*]. Yes, I—I agree.

HORTENSE. With which of us?

JEHANNE. Er—with both of you, of course. But—what were you wondering—about me, I mean?

HARRIET. Oh, nothing much. [*Curiosity conquering*] Only —has the King—er—kissed you yet?

JEHANNE [*starting*]. Kissed? Oh no! No, he hasn't. And I—oh, I suppose it's very bad and unpatriotic of me, but—but—you won't tell anyone if I tell you, will you?

HARRIET. We won't even whisper a word.

HORTENSE. For me, I never tell anyone anything.

JEHANNE. I don't want him to kiss me. You see, I—I've only been at Court a week and—and before I came—I live in the country, you know—my mother said, "Never let a married man kiss you, Jehanne." So I said I wouldn't, though I don't know why married men kiss any differently from single ones, do you?

HARRIET. What single ones have you been kissing?

JEHANNE. None at all. Why?

HORTENSE. Then how can you know anything about it?

JEHANNE. I don't! Please, I don't know anything about anything—and I wish the King wouldn't keep following me round and giving me roses and things. I'm not sure the Queen will like it.

HORTENSE [*dryly*]. You're *sure* you're not sure?

JEHANNE. Well, I'm afraid so. But I don't know what to do about it. It isn't my fault.

HARRIET. Except that you're a very pretty child.

JEHANNE. Oh, am I? Mother never told me that.

HORTENSE. I don't suppose she did.

JEHANNE. And then there's Lady Melisande, who seems quite to dislike me. She pinches me every time nobody's looking, and yesterday she said I was trying to cut her out with the King. I wondered whether she might be interested in him herself.

HARRIET. H'm!

JEHANNE. Do you think she is?

HARRIET. I wouldn't be surprised.

[*Melisande, a beautiful and imperious creature, enters R., regally.*

JEHANNE [*hastily*]. Here she comes! I—I think I'll go.

HARRIET [*hastily*]. No. You stay here and outface her, child. After all, you're as good as she is.

HORTENSE. A great deal better, I hope.

MELISANDE [*sweeping across to them*]. Were you talking about me?

HARRIET. Now why on earth should we be talking about you?

MELISANDE. You were. I know. [*To Jehanne*] You saucer-eyed little slut . . .

HARRIET. Now, now!

MELISANDE. And you two old gossips. When you get your heads together there's nothing harmless in your talk . . .

HORTENSE. But it doesn't follow that *you're* the only harmful thing for us to talk about, Melisande.

[*Ysabeau enters L.*

YSABEAU [*brightly*]. Hullo, Melisande. Quarrelling as usual?

MELISANDE. What do you mean—as usual?

YSABEAU. Oh, just the usual meaning, darling. [*To Hortense*] Have you had a nice—I mean, got a nice lot of winding done?

HORTENSE [*suddenly winding fast*]. Oh, quite a quantity.

MELISANDE [*to Jehanne*]. I've come after you.

JEHANNE [*scared*]. Me?

MELISANDE. I hear the King gave you a rose this morning, from the special tree in the middle of the rose garden.

JEHANNE. Yes. Wasn't it kind of him? [*Doubtfully*] But—ought I to have refused it, or something? I thought he wanted me to take it . . .

YSABEAU. He did.

MELISANDE. Of course you should have refused it. No self-respecting girl takes gifts from a married man.

JEHANNE. But I've never been offered any by a *single* man.

YSABEAU. And Lady Melisande is a great authority on what a self-respecting girl ought to do—because she's neither.

MELISANDE. How dare you!

HARRIET. Children, children!

MELISANDE. If I have any more of your cheek, Ysabeau, I'll smack your face. And you, Mistress Jehanne, all round-eyed innocence and the flavour of country turnips, let me tell you this: the roses on that tree are all mine. *Mine.* The King has no right to give them to anyone, much less to you. Why, he named that tree Melisande, after me.

JEHANNE. Oh, but—I'm really sorry, Melisande, but he can't have done that, because he's named it Jehanne, after me. He told me so, only this morning—and a rose-tree can't be called two names, can it?

YSABEAU. That particular rose-tree has been called a good many names in its time. [*Giggling*] Most of the names have gone home in a hurry.

JEHANNE [*dolefully*]. I wish I could go home—to Mother.

MELISANDE. So do I.

YSABEAU. Leave her alone, Melisande. You're jealous of her.

HORTENSE. I think you should both be ashamed of yourselves—taking the poor King away from the poor Queen.

HARRIET. And in two different directions at once, it seems.

JEHANNE. But I haven't—have I?

MELISANDE. Not for want of trying.

JEHANNE. Oh!

YSABEAU. Melisande, you cat!

MELISANDE. Cat yourself!   [Smacks Ysabeau's face.

YSABEAU. Oh!   [Smacks Melisande's face.

[*The Queen enters R. She is an impressive lady of middle-age, magnificently dressed, who tries to make dignity take the place of looks. Her movement is a sort of regal waddle. Melisande and Ysabeau, aware of her entrance, immediately pretend a game of smacking each other's hands, with more ferocity than is necessary. Harriet, Hortense, and Jehanne curtsy, Harriet and Hortense dropping their silk in doing so.*

QUEEN [*sitting*]. Are you two playing some sort of game—or what?

                    [*Melisande and Ysabeau swing round and curtsy.*

MELISANDE. ⎫
YSABEAU. ⎭ Your Grace . . .

QUEEN. Was it a game? Come, come now. Answer me.

MELISANDE. Yes, madam. We were playing "This year, next year . . ."

YSABEAU. "Sometime, never."

HARRIET [*foolishly butting in*]. "Catch a nigger by his toe . . ." Oh no, that's another one, isn't it? Or isn't it?

QUEEN. Must you refer to toes?

HARRIET. Oh, pardon, your Grace. I should have remembered. Er—how is the royal bunion this afternoon?

QUEEN. Royal bunion? There is no such thing. Haven't you been at Court long enough to know that, while as a woman I may suffer such afflictions, as a queen I have no feet?

HARRIET [*curtsying so hurriedly that she topples on to all fours*]. I stand corrected, madam.

[*Harriet covers her confusion by gathering up the silk.*

QUEEN. Now leave me—er, us—all of you. Except Jehanne. I want to talk to Jehanne.

JEHANNE [*miserably, curtsying*]. Yes, your Grace.

MELISANDE [*nastily*]. Oh!

QUEEN. What do you mean by that, Melisande?

MELISANDE. I said, "Oh!"

QUEEN. And meant?

MELISANDE. I meant that, if you aren't careful, this whey-faced little moon-gazing cow . . .

QUEEN. Melisande!

MELISANDE. . . . will be stealing the King's affections from where they properly belong.

QUEEN. Speaking for yourself, you should say "improperly belong." Speaking of me, you are impertinent. And, now I come to think of it, you've become more and more impertinent lately; far more impertinent than anyone else to whom the royal affections have—er—fleetingly strayed. I shall punish you. Let me see—ah, I have it! [*To Hortense*] Duchess Hortense-Marie . . .

HORTENSE. Madam?

QUEEN. You will see that the Lady Melisande has no roast quails for supper, no larks' tongues in aspic, no nightingales in honey. She may finish off the cold mutton.

HORTENSE. Yes, madam.

MELISANDE. I shall go straight to the King and complain——

QUEEN. I wouldn't bother, if I were you.

MELISANDE. He will be furious——

QUEEN. Probably. But not the way you think. You see, he gave me the idea. He said—now, let me see, exactly what did he say? Oh, I know! He said, "That young hussy Melisande is getting above herself lately. You were quite right, my dear; she wants taking down a peg. Give her cold

B

mutton for supper. I hate hash." Remarkably thoughtful man, his Grace.

MELISANDE. Oh!

> [*Melisande flounces off L. Ysabeau laughs.*

QUEEN. What are you laughing at?

YSABEAU. Nothing, your Grace—er—that is, only at his Grace's little joke.

QUEEN. When you have been at Court a few years longer you will perhaps learn that you must never laugh at royal pronouncements unless expressly bidden to do so through the medium of the Lord Chamberlain.

YSABEAU [*curtsying*]. Yes, madam.

QUEEN. Watch your behaviour. There is enough cold mutton, at a pinch, for two. Now leave me—er, us—alone with this young person.

> [*Ysabeau, Harriet, and Hortense curtsy and back off R. During the following scene Melisande peeps cautiously on from L. from time to time, interested.*]

Come here, child.

> [*Jehanne, very nervous, goes up to the Queen, curtsying.*]

Your name is Jehanne?

JEHANNE. If it please your Grace . . .

QUEEN. Whether it does or not, wench, whether it does or not, I didn't christen you. Now listen to me. You have been at Court five minutes . . .

JEHANNE. A week, madam.

QUEEN. Don't contradict. Five minutes, I said. And you are already, I am informed, pursuing the King, trying to attract his notice.

JEHANNE. No . . .

QUEEN. Yes. He has been seen in your company on several occasions. Therefore you must have been pursuing him. You know that the King can do no wrong.

JEHANNE. I—I've been taught so. But—oh, your Grace, I— I've wondered lately whether—there might be exceptions . . .

QUEEN. There are no exceptions in royalty, which is absolutely absolute. Now, you will admit that a flirtation between a married man and a woman not his wife, especially if the other woman is young and pretty, is very wrong indeed?

JEHANNE [*naïvely*]. Why is it worse when the other woman is young and pretty?   [*Pause. The Queen inflates angrily.*

QUEEN. Are you presuming, child, to *sauce* me?

JEHANNE [*terrified*]. Oh, no, no! No! Not at all, madam! Oh, your Grace, I don't mean anything at all wrong, I don't, really.

QUEEN. Listen. The King can do no wrong. The King is a married man. For a married man to flirt with another woman . . .   [*Significant pause.*

JEHANNE. Y-yes. Especially a young and pr-pr-pretty one . . .

QUEEN [*severely*]. Don't prompt me. For a married man to flirt with another woman is very wrong indeed. Therefore, if there is wrong and the King cannot do it, the other woman must have. That's logic. Is it quite clear?

JEHANNE. Oh, p-p-perfectly.

QUEEN. And what do you suppose should be done to the other woman?

JEHANNE. I d-don't know. D-does it depend on who she is?

QUEEN. Somewhat. Anyone of high rank may be beheaded. [*Jehanne jumps.*] But a person of lower rank—[*significantly*] your own father is a mere knight, I believe?—would have to be hanged.

JEHANNE. Hanged? My father? D-do you mean you want to h-h-hang my father?

QUEEN. No. You.

JEHANNE [*jumping again*]. Me? B-b-but—I—haven't d-d-done anything—at least, not anything much . . .

QUEEN. So, my wench, you think that enticing my husband away from me is nothing much?

JEHANNE [*desperately*]. B-but I didn't—I haven't! I—I mean —he came without b-b-being enticed and—and—oh, I mean —I don't know what I mean.

QUEEN. That seems obvious.

JEHANNE. I don't like his ch-chasing me about and g-g-giving me flowers and things. I've tried to stop him, but it m-makes no difference. Oh! I don't w-want to be h-h-hanged! Can't I go home to M-m-mother instead?

QUEEN. No use. He'd only follow you there. You see, it's only new maids of honour who attract—I mean, who are attracted to him, and neither of the young persons next on the list is—er—sufficiently good-looking to be attracted to him. [*Thoughtfully*] There's Couteau's daughter—squints, and that girl from Jellebois—far too fat, and young Louise Terrepom—so many things her best friend might tell her but doesn't. No, there's no other possible attractee in the prospective maids of honour until we come to little Rohais de Bouillon, and she's only ten yet, so it will be some time before she's eligible. So you see, you're in a strong position, and that's why I'm bound to make an example of you. I'm a reasonably patient woman, but you're the forty-eighth, and you must admit that four dozen is a lot . . . [*Jehanne has thrown herself on her knees and is sobbing. The Queen becomes aware of the fact and is mildly surprised.*] Why, what's the matter now?

JEHANNE. N-nothing, your Gr-gr-grace.

QUEEN [*kindly*]. There, there, child! You're very young and ignorant, and probably didn't realize what you were doing.

JEHANNE. Oh, indeed I didn't—whatever it was I did.

QUEEN. Perhaps we can stretch a point in your case——

JEHANNE [*gratefully*]. Oh, thank you! Thank you!

QUEEN. —and imagine that you are the daughter of a duke. Merely for the occasion, of course.

JEHANNE [*fearfully*]. What—occasion?

QUEEN. The execution. Then you can be done nicely with

full ceremonial and a sword. [*Jehanne flops again.*] That will be nice, won't it? You can wear your very best frock and it won't matter in the least about spoiling it. I always think a woman never really enjoys her best frock in ordinary circumstances, because she's so afraid of spilling things on it.

JEHANNE [*looking up, goggling, taking courage from despair*]. I —I want to make a suggestion——

QUEEN [*kindly*]. You'd better leave everything to me, dear. I'm really quite good at arranging these things—weddings and christenings and executions and so on. It will be quite a pretty show, quite pretty. I shall wear my cloth of silver and the emeralds. I do hope it will be fine.

JEHANNE. I can tell you a better way to stop the King being attracted by maids of honour—I mean, the maids of honour being attracted by the King—than by executing me.

QUEEN [*eagerly*]. What do you say? You've a better way of paying him—I mean, them—out?

JEHANNE. Yes. In your Grace's kitchens there are lots of girls as pretty as maids of honour.

QUEEN. That makes no difference. *Their* job is to cook.

JEHANNE. Have a young kitchen-wench up here. Wash her, dress her, teach her elocution and deportment . . .

QUEEN. Impossible.

JEHANNE. No. They learn quickly. After all, ours isn't nearly as hard a job as theirs.

QUEEN. Well, what then?

JEHANNE. Let the King know you've a new, young, and pretty maid of honour. He'll at once fall in love with her, and . . .

QUEEN. Hussy! Haven't I told you that . . .

JEHANNE. I mean, his Grace is so kind-hearted that he'll allow her to fall in love with him, and when he learns that he's allowed a mere kitchen-wench to fall in love with him he'll be so ashamed of himself—I mean, of her—that he'll never look at any woman again.

QUEEN. H'm-m-m!

JEHANNE [*afterthought*]. Oh, excepting your Grace, of course.

QUEEN [*dryly*]. Precisely. [*Thoughtfully*] It might work. [*Confidently*] It ought to work.

JEHANNE. It will work, madam.

QUEEN. Call a page.

JEHANNE [*going to door R., calling*]. Bastian!

[*Bastian enters and bows.*

QUEEN. Go down to the kitchens, boy, and fetch up the least *un*attractive of the serving wenches there.

BASTIAN. Immediately, your Grace? Or shall she be bathed first?

QUEEN. Bring her in her dirt. We want her at once.

BASTIAN. Yes, your Grace.

[*He bows and goes off R. The Queen, excited, begins to waddle to and fro across the stage, obliquely. Jehanne, tense, keeps her eyes solemnly fixed on the Queen, so that her head turns slowly from side to side as the Queen passes and repasses her. Each time the Queen catches Jehanne's eyes, both start. This goes on for a moment, in dead silence, with Melisande looking on now and then when the others cannot see her. Then Bastian enters R. and bows.*

BASTIAN. This, your Grace, is Alys.

[*Alys enters very nervously. She is a little kitchen-wench, very dirty, dressed in something like sacking, with bare feet. Her hair is hidden by a cloth tied over her head. Her mouth is partly open, which gives her a vacant expression, and her carriage and voice are bad. In her hands is a dishclout, which she twists and untwists nervously.*

QUEEN. So you are Alys?

ALYS [*bobbing awkwardly*]. Y-yes.

QUEEN. Yes, what?

ALYS [*giggling*]. Y-yes, please.

QUEEN. "Yes, *your Grace*."

ALYS. Yes, your Grace.

QUEEN [*sitting, regally*]. Now tell me, Alys, would you like to be a maid of honour? [*Alys looks very vacant.*] I mean, like this young lady here—to wear fine clothes . . .

ALYS [*giggling, eagerly*]. An' never do no work? Oh, *yes* mum.

QUEEN. Very well, you shall. [*To Jehanne*] Take her away and see they give her a bath—a thorough bath.

CURTAIN

SCENE II: THE FOLLOWING DAY

Music as at opening, repeated for a moment. The curtain rises. Hortense and Harriet are sitting on the bench, beginning to nod and lean on each other, but so far with all feet on the floor. Bastian is lounging R., amused. Ysabeau is sitting on the stool, laughing. Jehanne is trying to coach Alys, who, now clean, richly dressed, her hair visible, her expression no longer vacant, is seen to be a very lovely girl. She is trying to approach and curtsy to the Queen's chair, but she is still awkward and makes many mistakes which have reduced her nearly to tears as the scene opens.

JEHANNE. Alys! No, no, no! Not that way, I keep telling you. Like this. [*Demonstrates approach and sweeping curtsy.*] Now try again.

ALYS [*miserably*]. Y-yes, miss.

JEHANNE. Don't call me 'miss.' Remember that you're just as good as we are.

[*Hortense sits up with a jerk, frowning.*

HORTENSE. Kindly note that the royal ladies-in-waiting, the Duchess Harriet-Theodosie and myself, wish to dissociate ourselves from that statement. [*Nods again.*

HARRIET [*sleepily*]. I entirely disagree with you, Hortense-Marie. What statement was it, anyway? [*Nods again.*

JEHANNE [*taking no notice*]. You really must try, Alys.

ALYS. I be—am—trying.

YSABEAU. Buck up, Alys, or we'll have Lady Melisande back.

JEHANNE [*quickly, to Ysabeau*]. She mustn't know this. She'd give us away to the King. [*To Alys*] Now once again, Alys. Remember that the Queen is supposed to be sitting in that chair, and that, however disrespectful you may be below stairs, up here we have to be respectful—very respectful—to her.

ALYS. Oh dear! I d' wish I'd a-stayed in the kitchen.

JEHANNE [*correcting her*]. "I wish I'd stayed in the kitchen."

ALYS [*imitating Jehanne's more refined accent, but keeping her own words*]. I d' wish I'd a-stayed in the kitchen.

JEHANNE. No, no!

ALYS [*refined*]. But, miss, I'm sure as 'ow my voice sounded s' nice as what yours did.

JEHANNE [*sighing*]. Oh, dear! Well, one thing at a time. Come up again and curtsy to the Queen. Small steps, now. Take the skirt gracefully in each hand—no, gracefully, not with your fingers all bunched up. Remember that your hands are beautiful things and must always look beautiful. Slide the right foot round the left and behind it, and sink— sink, I said, not wobble.   [*Alys does a grotesque curtsy.*

YSABEAU. Don't wobble!

ALYS. I ain't wobbling.

JEHANNE. You are.

[*Business to continue for a moment, Alys doing everything wrong from wobbling to splits, and finally toppling over backward. Jehanne becomes irritated.*]

Oh, Alys! Please do *try*——

ALYS [*tearfully*]. I be trying.

JEHANNE [*correcting*]. "I *am* trying." [*Contradicting*] No, you're not.

ALYS [*annoyed, refined*]. Seem t' me as 'ow you don't know

yer own mind, miss. I be tired, anyway, an' I wishes as 'ow I'd never started on this yer wild-goose chase, that I does.

[*Alys blubbers. Ysabeau and Bastian laugh more.*
[*Jehanne, with a gesture of despair, runs off R. in tears. Ysabeau and Bastian abruptly stop laughing.*

YSABEAU [*concerned*]. Jehanne! ... Stop her, Bastian!

[*Bastian runs off R., followed by Ysabeau, leaving Alys still blubbering. Hortense and Harriet are too nearly asleep to take any notice. Melisande enters L., considers Alys maliciously for a moment, then nods, and, going to Alys, touches her shoulder.*

MELISANDE [*pretending kindness*]. What's the matter?

ALYS. Who are you?

MELISANDE. I'm Melisande. Who are you?

ALYS. I'm Alys.

MELISANDE. Oh, you're the little kitchen-wench they are having a joke with.

ALYS. Joke?

MELISANDE. Yes. I heard them planning it—the Queen and the ladies. They were to get you here, dress you up, and then make fun of you.

ALYS [*angrily*]. Make fun o' me?

MELISANDE. Yes. But—look here, I'll help you pay them out. You let me teach you to curtsy and things. I can do it, and in a week I'll make you as good as any of them. And you're much prettier.

ALYS. I'm not s' pretty as you.

MELISANDE. Oh yes, you are. You must have a good opinion of yourself, or you'll never get on in this world. When you've learned everything you'll be able to make fun of them, because the King will be sure to notice you, and that will make you the most important person in the whole palace.

ALYS. More important than the Queen?

MELISANDE. Oh, much.

ALYS. Shall I be able to order Cook about?

MELISANDE. Oh no. No one's important enough for that.
But you'll be able to order everyone else about.

ALYS. Do they really want to make fun of me?

MELISANDE. Of course they do. Why else do you suppose
they've got you here and dressed you up? Now come along
to my room, and I'll give you some lessons in private. Then
we'll show them who'll do the laughing.

[*Melisande sweeps off R. Alys hesitates for a moment, then
follows, with a laughable exaggeration of Melisande's
haughty manner. During the foregoing Hortense and
Harriet have gradually slipped into the positions they
occupied at the beginning of Scene I, and now they begin
gently to sway and snore. After a moment of this the scene
closes.*]

CURTAIN

SCENE III: A MONTH LATER

*Music as at opening, repeated for a moment. The curtain rises.
Hortense and Harriet have adopted a new position. They are
sitting uncomfortably on either end of the bench, facing inward,
their legs on the bench and along the length of it, their feet placed
together, sole to sole. They are still winding off a skein of silk,
which stretches between them.*

HARRIET. Well, one thing's quite certain. She's worse than
that impudent young hussy, Melisande, ever knew how to be.

HORTENSE. For the first time in my life, Harriet-Theodosie,
I am unreservedly in agreement with you. And it's a crying
shame that, at our time of life, we should be forced to agree
with each other.

HARRIET. Yes, Hortense-Marie.

HORTENSE. I should never have thought it possible that a
young person from the—actually from the lower regions—

should have acquired so many of the—er—graces of *our* state of life in so short a time—only a month! It makes one wonder.

HARRIET. Yes, indeed, it does. But what?

HORTENSE. What? *What* what?

HARRIET. What does it make one wonder?

HORTENSE. That should be perfectly obvious, Harriet-Theodosie, even to as big a fool as you are. It makes one wonder whether all the attributes of our breeding are merely a superficial veneer acquired with ease by the merest scullery wench.

HARRIET. But she was a kitchen-wench—a higher rank than the scullery.

HORTENSE. Don't stray from the point.

HARRIET. I can't stray anywhere, or I shall fall off here. This idea of yours for preventing yourself from dropping off to sleep is highly original but vastly uncomfortable, Hortense-Marie.

HORTENSE. To prevent *myself*? It's to prevent *you* from going to sleep. I *never* go to sleep.

HARRIET. Poor darling! How tired you must be! All your years and no sleep.

HORTENSE. I mean, during the daytime—dear.

HARRIET. Then why didn't you say so—dear?

[*Ysabeau and Jehanne enter R., sadly.*

YSABEAU. Look at them. A month ago I'd have laughed to split my ribs—but there isn't a laugh left in me now.

[*Hortense and Harriet get their feet down to the floor, awkwardly.*

JEHANNE. When I think of what that little wretch Alys has developed into, I—I wish I'd *let* the King flirt with me, Mother's advice or no Mother's advice. Why, I'd sooner have been beheaded—almost.

YSABEAU. The joke's certainly against us. Why, she's started to treat even the Queen like a servant.

JEHANNE. And the King's so infatuated with her he lets her

do exactly as she wants. It's not a bit of good suggesting that she was a kitchen-wench. He won't believe it, now.

YSABEAU. No. We pitched the tale too well in the first place about her ancestry. That's the worst of telling lies.

[*Bastian enters R.*

BASTIAN [*loudly, seriously*]. I am commanded to proclaim the latest royal decree. His Grace the King has ordained that anyone speaking against the Duchess Alys, even though it be no more than a whisper . . .

[*Hortense and Harriet spring to their feet, together.*

HORTENSE. A duchess now, is she? This is too much!

HARRIET. Much too much!

BASTIAN. . . . shall be deemed guilty of treasonable utterance and shall suffer a felon's death upon the galace pallows—I beg your pardon!—the palace gallows. God save the King!

[*To Hortense and Harriet, who have deflated.*]
Did you say anything?

HORTENSE.⎫
⎬Us? No. We never said a word.
HARRIET.⎭

BASTIAN. I'm sorry to hear it. You'd look sweet, dangling side by side like a couple of over-ripe pears.

HARRIET [*to Hortense*]. Did you hear that? He called you an over-ripe pear.

HORTENSE. No. It was you he meant. But what insolence! Why, even I have never called you an over-ripe pear, have I?

HARRIET. You'd better not try.

HORTENSE. Harriet-Theodosie! After all our years of perfect friendship are we going to quarrel *again*?

YSABEAU. Oh, be quiet, you two! We must unite in face of a common enemy.

JEHANNE. If only we could *do* something! That insufferable little cat——

[*Alys enters R. She is now very beautiful, self-assured, and imperious. She sweeps up to the Queen's chair and sits. The Ladies curtsy to her, and Bastian bows.*

ALYS [*coldly*]. Did I hear something about a cat?

YSABEAU [*promptly*]. Yes. The wretched animal never was properly house-trained.

ALYS. And no more were you. I have decided that you shall have a little education in something really useful this morning.

HORTENSE.
HARRIET. } S-something—really—useful—— ?
YSABEAU.
JEHANNE.

ALYS. You've never done anything the least bit useful all your lives.

[*The Queen, a sadder and wiser woman, enters R. quite diffidently. Hortense and Harriet begin to curtsy, but straighten up hastily at an angry gesture from Alys.*]

QUEEN [*to Bastian*]. Ah, here you are, boy! I've been looking for you. I want you to go and pick me some roses.

ALYS. That is impossible. I want him here.

QUEEN. Oh, I beg your pardon.

ALYS. Besides, all those roses are mine. The King has named all the trees after me. [*To Bastian*] Go to the kitchens, boy, and bring the apples and the bowl of dough.

QUEEN. Kitchens?

HORTENSE. Apples?

HARRIET. Dough?

QUEEN.
HORTENSE. } Here ?
HARRIET.

[*Bastian has bowed and gone off R. Melisande, somewhat subdued now, enters L. and goes up to Alys.*]

MELISANDE. You've really come on wonderfully, my dear.

ALYS [*coldly*]. Come on wonderfully?

MELISANDE. But you must admit I'm a good teacher.

ALYS [*turning her back*]. I haven't the slightest idea what you mean. And kindly remember to speak when you are spoken to and not before.

MELISANDE [*starting*]. Oh!

> [*Bastian enters R. with a bowl of dough and another of apples on a small table, which he sets down C. He has also a folded pinafore under his arm.*

ALYS. Now you are going to learn how to make an apple-pie.

QUEEN.
HORTENSE.
HARRIET. } An—apple-pie——
JEHANNE.
YSABEAU.

MELISANDE. I am not.

ALYS [*to Melisande*]. The King's latest decree is that anyone who refuses to obey my orders shall be hanged.

BASTIAN. On the galace pallows—I beg your pardon!—the palace gallows. God save the King!

MELISANDE. Oh!

ALYS [*to Melisande*]. Which reminds me that you have not curtsied to me this morning. Where are your manners?

> [*Melisande curtsies sullenly.*]

That needs improvement. I shall have to give you some lessons. [*To the others*] Now, you must give your minds to this apple-pie, because I am making new arrangements here. You are all going to change places with the domestic staff, turn and turn about.

QUEEN [*indignantly*]. What? [*Alys glares at her.*] I—I mean, I beg your pardon. I'm afraid my hearing isn't what it was, and——

ALYS. For one month the domestic staff will be maids of honour, and you will be serving wenches. Then for the next month you will change about. That will make everyone really useful. At present a kitchen-wench would be hopelessly at a loss if she were presented at Court——

MELISANDE. But she wouldn't be presented at Court——

ALYS [*truculently*]. Why not? . . . And, on the other hand, a maid of honour would be a perfect fool trying to make herself, say, a rice pudding.

YSABEAU. But who wants rice pudding?

ALYS. Be quiet.

QUEEN [*doubtfully*]. I don't want to sound—er—disapproving, but—er—isn't it—er—rather a revolutionary idea?

ALYS. All new ideas are revolutionary. That's why you people in the comfortable classes never encourage new ideas.

QUEEN. Well, I suppose, if you want to teach them—this apple-thing, I mean—you'd better get on with it.

ALYS. I shall begin with you.

QUEEN [*starting*]. Me? But—but—look here, young woman —I—I mean, of course, my *dear* Duchess—I've quite enough to do, being Queen.

ALYS. Oh, but you won't be Queen, then. You'll be cook.

QUEEN. C-c-c-c——

ALYS. Not so much because of any possible ability you may have—in fact, I've no opinion at all of your ability—but because you've the likeliest figure.

QUEEN [*furiously*]. Oh! This is more than flesh and blood will stand—especially royal flesh and blood! I won't do it! D'you hear, I won't!

ALYS [*calmly*]. Speaking to his Grace this morning about the new law, I said, "I suppose I can hang *anyone* who disobeys?" And he said "Yes." And I said, "Even including the Queen?" And he said, "Yes, of course—but that's too much to hope for."

[*Pause. The Queen is furious, opens her mouth to say something rude about the King, changes her mind and closes it, then becomes frightened.*

QUEEN. Oh, all right, all right! I'll learn. What do I do?

ALYS [*to Bastian*]. Put on her pinafore.

[*Bastian envelops the Queen in a large pinafore. There is comic business during this, the Queen giggling and wriggling as he inadvertently tickles her, then stopping suddenly at a severe glance from Alys.*]

Now roll up your sleeves.

QUEEN [*as she does so, making the best of it*]. After all, a cook is really far more important than a queen.

ALYS. If I hear any more such remarks I'll make you a scullery wench.

QUEEN. Oh dear, dear! What do I do now?

ALYS. Knead.

QUEEN. Need? I need a lot of things, but——

ALYS. Knead the dough. Put your hands into it and work it about.

> [*The Queen does so, with humorous results, getting thoroughly involved with long strings of sticky dough. The others watch, too dejected to laugh. Suddenly the Queen looks up to where the window is or is imagined to be, pointing excitedly with a doughy hand.*

QUEEN [*joyfully*]. Look!   [*All except Alys crowd to look.*

ALYS [*sharply*]. Get back to your places. [*To the Queen*] You get on with your work.

QUEEN. The King——

YSABEAU. With another girl——

JEHANNE. He's picking a rose for her——

MELISANDE [*triumphantly to Alys*]. He's pretty soon forgotten you. I lasted at least a fortnight longer——

> [*Alys sits still, saying nothing.*

BASTIAN. She isn't one of the palace ladies.

HORTENSE. } I wonder who she can be.
HARRIET.

QUEEN. Not one of the palace ladies? Has he started going outside for his—er—amusements, then? There'll be no end to this, if he's the whole city to choose from. [*Going to the bowl and taking all the dough between her hands, purposefully*] I'll see to him—and her! [*Runs off L., carrying the dough.*

ALYS. Come back!

MELISANDE [*dangerously, going to Alys*]. You don't seem to understand what this means to you.

ALYS. But the King made a new law——

MELISANDE. Which he's forgotten already, as he's forgotten you. Come on, girls! We'll deal with her.

HORTENSE [*primly*]. Are you calling me a girl?

MELISANDE. Put us in the kitchens, would she? That's how she repays me for teaching her to be a lady!

HARRIET. It seems you didn't, anyway.

MELISANDE. What shall we do with her?

YSABEAU [*looking off, laughing*]. Just look what the Queen's doing with the King! I shouldn't have thought that dough would have gone so far.

JEHANNE [*joining her, laughing*]. Doesn't he look funny?

BASTIAN [*peering over their shoulders, laughing*]. And the—er—lady's taken to her heels.

HARRIET [*peering*]. I wish my eyesight were better.

HORTENSE. You always were inquisitive, Harriet-Theodosie. [*Eagerly*] What is going on, anyway?

> [*She tries to look over or round the others.*

MELISANDE. Never mind them. Let's settle with this one.

ALYS. You needn't bother. We're settled now.

MELISANDE. *Are* we?

ALYS. Oh yes. You all had me here for a joke—a rather cruel joke, I think. I managed to turn it back on you, that's all.

YSABEAU. Joke?

ALYS. You got me here and decked me up as a maid of honour, only to make fun of me. I think that was very unkind.

JEHANNE. But we didn't——

ALYS. But you did. This one here—the stuck-up one—told me so.

JEHANNE.
YSABEAU. } Melisande told you that? The little——
HARRIET.
HORTENSE.

> [*Bastian holds up a hand for silence, interrupting them.*

BASTIAN [*bowing to Alys*]. The ladies have the honour to

C

inform you that the Lady Melisande seldom, if ever, speaks the truth.

JEHANNE [*to Alys*]. I suggested having you up here, not to make fun of you, but to cure the King of chasing maids of honour.

ALYS. How?

JEHANNE. Well—er—I thought that, if you were properly dressed and—all that—he wouldn't know the difference, and when he found out he'd been chasing a——

ALYS [*suspiciously*]. What difference?

YSABEAU [*hastily*]. Let me explain—Jehanne's not doing it very well. It's like this—we're all very soft, really; not much good for anything, any of us, even for discouraging a king. We thought that you, with your additional experience——

ALYS [*suspiciously*]. What experience?

YSABEAU [*hastily continuing*]. —and intelligence—especially intelligence, would be able to deal satisfactorily with him.

ALYS [*to Harriet*]. Is this true?

HARRIET. Oh yes! Yes! Quite! I'm not a bit of good at discouraging kings. I never discouraged one in my life.

HORTENSE. Not that that ever made the slightest difference, Harriet-Theodosie.   [*Harriet bridles. Alys begins to laugh.*

ALYS. And I've been deliberately unpleasant to you all, because I thought you were being unkind to me.

MELISANDE. I wasn't.

ALYS. Oh, I just didn't like your manners—the only thing, apparently, you were truthful about.

MELISANDE [*angrily*]. How dare you! [*To the others*] Come on, throw her out!

YSABEAU. You're the one to be thrown out.

JEHANNE. Yes.

[*Ysabeau, Jehanne, and Bastian close in on Melisande, who tries in vain to escape. Harriet and Hortense dither round them like scared hens. There is a general scuffle, only Alys remaining outside it, standing before the chair. Then Melisande breaks away and runs L.*

YSABEAU. Don't let her go!

[Melisande is stopped in the entrance by the Queen, who still wears the pinafore, into the top of which is stuck a rose. The Queen enters, slapping the remains of the dough off her hands with an air of great satisfaction.

QUEEN. That's a job well done!

[She sweeps Melisande before her to C., otherwise ignoring her, then takes the rose from her pinafore with a flourish.]

It may have appeared to you young ladies——

HARRIET *[nudging Hortense].* Did you hear? She's talking to us, too——

QUEEN *[to Harriet].* Get on with your winding, you two.

[Harriet and Hortense start and hastily collect their skein and ball, getting thoroughly mixed up with it, and finishing downstage R. and L. respectively, the silk stretching the width of the stage between them as they feverishly wind it.]

It may have appeared to you ladies that I am both blind and a fool——

YSABEAU *[hastily].* Oh no, your Grace. We never for one moment imagined that you are *blind*.

QUEEN *[mollified, smiling].* Ah! *[Smile wiped out, suddenly suspicious.]* What? *[Stares at Ysabeau, then continues]* But I can assure you that I am not quite such a fool as I look.

JEHANNE *[innocently].* Of course not, your Grace. *[The Queen glares, Jehanne starts.]* Oh dear! Have I said something wrong?

QUEEN. Oh, let it pass! Let it pass!

MELISANDE *[curtsying].* I want to complain, your Grace. They were ill-treating me——

QUEEN. I don't want to know what they were doing. Whatever it was, you deserved it. Anyway, it's nothing to what I'm going to do with you.

MELISANDE. What?

QUEEN [*on dais, standing before her chair*]. I know all about you.

MELISANDE [*indicating Alys*]. What about her?

QUEEN. I know all about her, too. [*Patting Alys*] A good girl, Alys, if a little—er—unusual in her methods. She's staying here with me, to help keep the King in order. You're going down to the kitchens for a week's training in good behaviour.

MELISANDE. If you think I'm going to be a cook——

QUEEN. You're not. You're going to wash dishes.

MELISANDE [*furiously*]. I've never taken orders from you, and I'm not going to now.

QUEEN [*twirling the rose*]. Oh, aren't you? Do you know what this is called? The King has just named it Clemence-Olympe-Hippeastra—[*She giggles and simpers on the last words, holding the rose against her lower lip. The others, except Melisande, begin to chuckle, the chuckles expanding into laughter. The Queen looks puzzled for a moment, then suddenly becomes angry. Instantly the laughter stops, the ladies curtsy, and Bastian bows. The Queen glares imperiously at Melisande, pointing at the floor before her feet, and Melisande also curtsies. Then a large smile of satisfaction appears on the Queen's face as she poses triumphantly*]—after me.

CURTAIN

CHECK TO THE QUEEN

by T. B. Morris

CHARACTERS

MARY HOWARD
BRIDGET MANNERS   } maids of honour
ELIZABETH THROCKMORTON
MARY RADCLIFFE, *lady-in-waiting*
ELIZABETH, *Queen of England*

CHECK TO THE QUEEN

THE SCENE: *A room in Whitehall Palace.*

A curtain set, or stone walls hung with tapestries. Essential properties: a chair for the Queen, two or three joint-stools, and a pile of cushions for the maids, and a small table with a set of chessmen and board on it. Additional properties at pleasure: a chest or court cupboard, books, manuscripts, a lute, appropriate flowers in suitable vases. One entrance only may be used, if desired, and the stage may be arranged to the producer's convenience, so long as the table and chair are towards opposite ends of it. Actually the piece may be produced almost anywhere, without a stage and in a small room, as it is of an intimate nature and its action takes little space.

Tudor music before the rise of the curtain. The music may continue for a few moments after the curtain has risen, to allow the audience to appreciate the picture made by Howard and Manners, who are sitting on joint-stools to either side of the table, playing chess. Both are young girls, Manners the younger. Howard is a gay and mischievous little creature, Manners demure and charming. Howard cannot concentrate on the game for long, but must break off to gossip.

HOWARD. The Queen was loth to let Sir Walter go. In the end he had to appeal to her love of money. For the sake of her purse she'd send anyone anywhere, so now Raleigh is [*gesturing*] off to the ends o' the world—to that Eldorado he was for ever talking of. [*Impressively*] Mark me, milady Bridget, there's no one loves the colour of gold more than the Queen.

MANNERS [*laughing gently*]. In playing chess one does not think of royalty *off* the board.

[*Takes a piece or two from Howard.*

HOWARD. Ah! Fool to be chattering! I do no better than milord North, who ever loses to the Queen at primero—though I vow she cheats. 'Tis fortunate there are no ryalls to be lost on this. [*Manners takes another piece.*] 'Slight! You are a skilful player, Bridget.

MANNERS. Or you unskilful, milady Mary Howard. This is not how your great namesake scattered Philip's armada.

HOWARD. I must pay straiter attention. [*Concentrates for a moment, but soon gossips again.*] There is one who will soak her pillow for Raleigh's going.

MANNERS [*looking up*]. Many will regret him, and wish him safe return. A grand gentleman, if a little—overbold, perhaps.

HOWARD. Overbold? Marry! one needs have much boldness to climb to so dizzy a perch as Queen's favourite—[*significantly*] for all that she gave him a good hand up; a right royal hand, in sooth, that lifts—and grasps.

MANNERS [*seriously*]. Favourite? Do you mean that Sir Walter is the Queen's lover?

HOWARD [*giggling*]. Who shall say? . . . We have our eyes, and her Grace is never prudent overlong. But, whether he is or no, 'tis certain she will not allow of his sweethearting with anyone else.

MANNERS. You mean—Mistress Throckmorton? Though but new come to Court, I have observed——

HOWARD [*interrupting*]. Aha! So you know, too, whose tears keep her awake o' nights? Well, Raleigh will sail to his Eldorado, and Bess Throckmorton will forget him if she's any sense. Raleigh has a pleasant taste in doublets, and is to be thanked for this new fashion of burning the tobacco—I must try it when I can come by a smoking-pipe, though I have heard 'tis apt to be something disturbing to the stomachs of our sex.

MANNERS [*shuddering*]. A horrid custom.

HOWARD. Raleigh can turn a pretty line o' verse, and draw pretty eyes—but the Queen may have him, or Bess Throckmorton either, for me. His voice is thick with the Devon country he comes from.

MANNERS. I'd rather be in the country than here at Court.

HOWARD. What?

MANNERS. 'Tis noisy here, and quarrelsome. [*Ruefully*] And her Grace's hand can be heavy sometimes.

HOWARD. I' faith, it can! [*Impulsively*] Listen! I hate her Grace.

MANNERS [*astonished*]. Hate? But—the Queen——

HOWARD. Queen she may be [*rising*] and doubtless well enough as a ruler—with Burghley's arm to lean on——

MANNERS. *Well enough?* That does no justice to so great a sovereign. You are jesting, milady Howard.

HOWARD. Oh, call me Mary. I like you—or I'd not have told you that. We'll be great friends——

MANNERS. But I like not your—jests. And—I think it not wise to use such talk.

HOWARD [*lightly*]. As to that, a discreet indiscretion is the gear for this life. [*Bitterly*] 'Tis as woman I mislike her Grace. We can do nothing for her ruling and interference. She is old, painted. Her teeth are rotten and she wears a wig. Yet she persists in jetting herself as the paragon of all beauty; centre for the adoration of every personable young man who may come within her clutches. *She* is ever the sun, and we, the stars, may not shine for her. 'Slife! 'Tis all the seven sins rolled into one to do so much as fall in love here.

MANNERS. I am in no concern about love.

HOWARD. I should think not, i' faith, and you so near the cradle. But wait awhile, and you will be. [*Hesitating, then confiding*] I am.

MANNERS. You? I had not known——

HOWARD. I do not shout it through my eyes like poor,

forlorn Mistress Throckmorton. . . . Can you keep a secret?
Shall I tell you?

MANNERS [*quickly, uneasily*]. No, no! I want not to know
secrets of that kind. I must remember my good uncle's
counsel.

HOWARD. Your uncle?

MANNERS. He writ me a letter when I came to Court.

HOWARD [*laughing*]. The old are ever giving counsel to the
young—of all they, when young, refrained from.

MANNERS. Nay, 'tis good counsel. You shall hear it.
[*Takes from her bodice a creased parchment, and reads*] ". . . that
you apply yourself wholly to the service of her Majesty with
all meekness, love, and obedience——"

HOWARD. One might think he had never known her
Majesty——

MANNERS [*continuing*]. "—wherein you must be diligent,
secret, and faithful. To your elders and superiors, of reverent
behaviour; to your equals and fellow-servants, civil and
courteous; to your inferiors you must show all favour and
gentleness. *Generally that you be no meddler in the causes of
others.* That you use much silence, for that becometh maids,
especially of your calling. That your speech and endeavours
ever tend to the good of all and to the hurt of none. . . ."![1]
[*She stops, hurt, for Howard is in fits of laughter.*

HOWARD [*mimicking*]. That you be no *meddler* in the causes
of others! That you use *much* silence! Oh, 'tis rich! And
did your most worthy uncle pour out these vapourings to a
woman or a joint-stool?

MANNERS [*putting letter away*]. 'Tis a beautiful letter, and
you, milady Howard, are nothing but a pert hoyden to laugh
so at it.

HOWARD [*good-naturedly, putting an arm about Manners*].
There, poppet! I had no intent of hurting you. Indeed, by

[1] Copy of part of an actual letter to Lady Bridget Manners, but with
spelling modernized for convenience.

m'life! 'tis a beautiful letter—though 'tis pity 'tis so far above the capacity of a maiden to compass.

> [*Throckmorton, who has dark hair and eyes, and is rather older than the others, though still young, enters behind them, carrying a small piece of embroidery. For the moment she is unobserved by Howard and Manners.*

MANNERS. I shall endeavour to compass it.

HOWARD. Ay, and so you will, I'll warrant me! . . . *until you fall in love, and the Queen has word of it.*

MANNERS [*seriously*]. Is she truly so dreadful?

HOWARD [*confidentially, a little fearfully*]. Thirty years ago, milady Catherine Grey went to the Tower. Since then, her sister Mary and Lettice Knollys were forbidden the Court. Milady Sheffield, Mary Shelton, and Dorothy Devereux were disgraced—and there are others. A long list of disgraces, fallings, and sufferings—ay, and deaths too, for some broke their hearts of it—all for loving without her Grace's permission, which is never given but as a miser parts with gold, or *against her Grace's interest*. And her Grace has many—interests.

MANNERS. She is so—jealous?

HOWARD. She would not marry when she might—and now, love being out of her reach, she grudges it to others.

MANNERS. Why did she never marry?

HOWARD. Some say because she would not share her power with any man. And some say because she must have *all* men for ever worshipping her. And [*awed*] there are some who whisper—but say to none I told you this—that the fear her mother, Nan Bullen, was in at her birth, knowing King Henry was wearied of all but the notion of a *son* from her, bred in our Queen a horror of marriage, with yet a tormenting impulse thereto.

THROCKMORTON [*quietly*]. That is not true, Mary. Her Grace has kept all her heart for England.

> [*Howard and Manners swing round, startled.*

HOWARD. Why, Bess—I had not heard you, you mouse.

[*Throckmorton crosses to a pile of cushions and sits, beginning to work. She is quiet and sad.*]

And you know very well that the Queen serves her own purpose in all things.

THROCKMORTON. You must not, out of your experiences of the privy chamber and your own frivolities, judge of her appearance to the world. Do not forget that she is the Queen of England—no small thing, nowadays.

HOWARD [*mocking*]. Vastly serious this morning, Bess. I wonder why? [*Quotes lightly*]

> If all the world and love were *young*,
> And *truth* in every shepherd's tongue,
> These pretty pleasures might me move
> To live with thee and be thy love.

Only he's not a shepherd, is he, Bess? . . . But does he speak true?

THROCKMORTON. Is this a riddle?

HOWARD. Ay, for the heart. Sir Walter makes pretty verses, and whispers flatteries to a great lady—loud enough for a lady not so great to hear.

THROCKMORTON. What do you mean?

HOWARD. And now Sir Walter goes adventuring to the golden lands beyond the sunset, and ladies great and not so great may whistle awhile for him. [*Laughs and pirouettes about the room, singing*]

> John, come kiss me now,
> John, come kiss me now,
> John, come kiss me,
> Sweet, come kiss me,
> Make no more ado.

[*Throws open her arms invitingly, and stops, breathless, laughing.*

THROCKMORTON [*coldly*]. Milady Mary Howard is pleased to be pert this morning. [*Returning to her work*] Well, 'tis nothing unusual.

HOWARD. And Mistress Throckmorton is sad and sulky, which is vastly unusual. Do you love him so much, Bess?

THROCKMORTON. Love—who?

HOWARD. Well! Of all the brazen outfacings! Who has been kissing you in the pleached alleys, in the orchards and the shrubberies, in every secret corner o' the palace?

THROCKMORTON [*jumping up*]. Where heard you this? [*Recovering a little*] 'Tis a lie!

HOWARD. Aha! Little birds always tell tales—and their tales are nearly always true.

THROCKMORTON [*hitting back*]. A little bird called *Robin*, I suppose.

MANNERS [*awed*]. Robin? Milord of Essex? [*To Howard, fearfully*] Is it Essex you love?

HOWARD [*furiously*]. Mind your uncle's counsel, Bridget, and keep t' your own affairs.

THROCKMORTON. Essex, yes. All the world knows it, save the Queen. And Essex a married man, and——

HOWARD [*interrupting, sweetly acid*]. And rival, you would say, for the Queen's affections, with Sir Walter Raleigh—whom you know rather over-well, Mistress Bess.

[*For a moment Howard and Throckmorton face each other like cats about to spring.*

MANNERS [*fearfully*]. Mary—Bess—remember where you are——

HOWARD [*recovering, laughing*]. I' faith! here's milady Bridget Manners, newest come to Court, reading us a lesson in behaviour—all from her good uncle's words o' wisdom. [*To Throckmorton*] There! I'm sorry I teased you, Bess. If only you were not so serious and so—faithful. You should take a leaf from her Grace's book, and wear your lovers on a string.

[*Throckmorton sits again, quietly, not replying, and goes on with her work. Howard looks at her with some concern, then draws Manners across to the table.*]

Come, Bridget, we will finish our game. [*Quietly*] This has bitten deep in her.

[*For a moment they continue to play chess, while Throckmorton works, not looking up. Howard gives a curious glance or two at her, and once Throckmorton stealthily dabs her eyes. Then Radcliffe enters. She is middle-aged, rather prim but kindly, more soberly dressed than the others. She carries a large piece of embroidery, silks, etc.*]

RADCLIFFE. Work for your hands, maidens.

HOWARD [*saucily*]. Ah, Mistress Radcliffe, what else, when you appear? [*She and Manners rise and move their stools towards C., leaving the chessmen on the board.*] Well, I must e'en leave my victory over milady Bridget for another day.

MANNERS [*laughing*]. Victory? Mistress Radcliffe has saved you from defeat.

RADCLIFFE [*dryly, overlooking the chessboard*]. She has your king checked, milady Howard.

MANNERS. Well, the king must give way to the Queen's business.

HOWARD [*shrugging*]. As ever.

RADCLIFFE [*spreading out the embroidery*]. There is this pattern of grapes and pomegranates to finish [*or whatever the pattern is*]. Her Grace has a sudden desire for it.

HOWARD. Which she will forget to-morrow.

RADCLIFFE [*to Manners, ignoring this*]. You take this corner, child. And you [*to Howard*] the pattern here. [*Giving silks, etc.*] Mistress Throckmorton, the other side. What were you working?

THROCKMORTON [*listlessly, displaying it*]. But a kerchief for myself.

RADCLIFFE. A very pretty piece. You have a sweet touch

with colours, Bess. Perhaps you would give an eye to this child here [*indicating Manners*]. She is not yet——

[*Pauses, chuckling kindly.* ·

MANNERS [*gently*]. Say I am all promise and no performance, good Mistress Radcliffe. But I shall learn.

[*Howard, Manners, and Throckmorton are now sitting, working on the large embroidery. Radcliffe stands watching them, holding Throckmorton's kerchief.*

RADCLIFFE. To be sure you will.

MANNERS. I think I am learning. My mother said I was of no use for anything except a little playing of the lute, and that I stooped my shoulders. She was ashamed lest I should stoop at Court.

RADCLIFFE. You have grown out of that already.

HOWARD [*mischievously*]. But see you stoop not to folly—as women do. 'Tis difficult not to, in such a grand assembly of men.

RADCLIFFE. Now, milady Mary, take care o' your tongue. You are ever too free with it. And, as for men—popinjays, all o' them, thinking they shall be valued by the fortunes they bear on their backs; their bumbastings and quiltings, monstrous padded shoulders and thighs, and straitened waists like women; their jewelled cloaks and sugared sonnets—pah!

HOWARD [*to Manners*]. Mistress Radcliffe cannot abide men. I can't think how she managed for a father.

[*Howard and Manners laugh. Radcliffe chuckles.*

RADCLIFFE. S'sh! There is ever too much noise and heying about here, and was always. To bring young maids together is to bring foolishness to life.

HOWARD [*to Manners*]. Know you what happened when Mistress Radcliffe was a girl? Sir Francis Knollys had a room next the maids' dormitory——

RADCLIFFE. Nay, 'twas before my time.

HOWARD. The maids were used to frisk about and make much noise as they retired.

RADCLIFFE. As they have done ever since.

HOWARD. Sir Francis made many protests, vainly, until one night when their merriment was high he [*laughing*] stalked into their room in nothing but his shirt and spectacles, reading a book. There were they, in—er—little else but great confusion, and he for a whole hour paced gravely up and down, reading, with the poor creatures not knowing which way to turn nor what to do. [*Howard and Manners laugh.*

RADCLIFFE [*warning*]. S'sh! Do not disturb her Grace. I am not sure of her mood this morning, but I think she has not shaken off yesterday's glumness.

HOWARD. The Court is dull for her without Sir Walter.

[*Throckmorton, who has been working in silence, stiffens. Radcliffe observes this.*

RADCLIFFE. You are quiet this morning, Bess. [*Kindly*] Why not sing something as you work? Her Grace approves your voice, which is more than I can say for some.

THROCKMORTON. No, I—I am not in the mood.

[*Elizabeth is heard, off, at a little distance, singing a merry Tudor song.*

HOWARD. Well, there is one who is.

RADCLIFFE [*surprised*]. The Queen. She is merrier than I had thought.

HOWARD. Much thanks for that.

MANNERS. She is coming here.

[*Manners, Howard, and Throckmorton rise. The singing draws nearer, then Queen Elizabeth enters. She is 57, elaborately painted, bewigged, gorgeously dressed and wearing many jewels, carrying a fan. In a gay mood, she continues a snatch of her song. The others curtsy. She gestures them up, laughing.*

RADCLIFFE. Your Grace is in good voice this morning.

ELIZABETH. Well enough. I have been better.

HOWARD [*flattering*]. 'Tis sweet, your Grace.

MANNERS. Sweet, indeed.

ELIZABETH [*who loves flattery*]. And what think you, Mistress Throckmorton?

THROCKMORTON [*making an effort*]. Your Grace does nothing that is not excellent.

ELIZABETH [*delighted*]. Pleasantly said. [*Taking Throckmorton's kerchief from Radcliffe*] Whose work is this?

RADCLIFFE. Bess, here, is working it.

ELIZABETH. And very beautiful work, in sooth! [*Determined to have it*] A sweet thought, Bess, to work it for me. I'll have six o' the pattern, and you may give them to me at next New Year.

THROCKMORTON [*making the best of it, curtsying*]. I—shall be honoured.

ELIZABETH [*touching Throckmorton's cheek affectionately*]. There, there! A good child! You are something pale this morning, Bess. You are pining for the country in this golden weather?

THROCKMORTON. Being near your Grace, how can I need more?

ELIZABETH. Well said again, wench! And you shall have your country for a while.

THROCKMORTON [*suddenly hopeful*]. I will confess I should like to see my home for—a little.

ELIZABETH [*sharply*]. Your home? Nay, I meant not that. I cannot spare you from my side. We go on progress. [*Throckmorton tries to hide her disappointment. Elizabeth sits and continues, forgetting her,*] This London of ours is a great and a glorious place, but in the heat one is best out o' the stink of it —a matter that our citizens are overlong in setting to rights. We shall have more o' the plague if 'tis not sweetened—but there, that is London. All colour and pageantry overhead, rottenness underfoot. So we'll progress to the fresh country, and let our good people there rejoice in us for a while.

RADCLIFFE. That were good for you, madam.

ELIZABETH. For me? Better for them. You know well,

Radcliffe, 'tis small easing o' labour for me. An' I overlook not all arrangements to the smallest o' them, all goes awry. You have noted it. There is not enough plate, so that I must travel like a pauper, or the beer is sour, so that the Court gasps like a netful o' fish.   [*Laughs.*

HOWARD. Your servants are fortunate in a wise mistress.

ELIZABETH [*brusquely*]. Who does their work for them, most on't. [*Pointing*] Have a care t' those colours, Mary Howard. They sort together no better than France and Spain.

    [*Radcliffe and Howard put their heads together anxiously over the embroidery, miming a whispered consultation.*

MANNERS [*shyly*]. But your Majesty has accounted for Spain.

ELIZABETH. We ha' given Philip a shrewd knock, but Spain is still on the horizon wi' the storm-clouds, and Europe a quicksand o' treachery, shivering now this way and now that. This England is but a small speck of earth, for whose safety we may thank the seas.

RADCLIFFE. And our ships that hold the seas, madam.

ELIZABETH. We must ha' more ships, and yet more ships. That is what my father said, and that is what I say—and I am right, as all the world shall see. We shall speak louder in the affairs o' the world. [*Rising, continuing immediately*] Come with me, Mary. I need your help in the choice of a dress for the masque to-night. Shall I wear the green satin, with the embroidery of roses and mulberries in Venice gold, and the new ruff of cobweb lace and emeralds? Or the marigold velvet slashed with crimson, and the pearl ruff?

RADCLIFFE. I will attend your Grace. With so many dresses, and all becoming you so well——

HOWARD. Mistress Radcliffe would say that you add grace to all, madam.

ELIZABETH [*pleased*]. Yet would I had a man's opinion on such matters of weight. Essex is of little use. He can no more give an opinion on a dress than he can turn a compliment

D

on a face. [*Lightly, almost giggling*] Raleigh is his master in both.

RADCLIFFE. Sir Walter will be away from Chatham to-morrow, an' his matters have gone well.

[*Elizabeth is going off. Howard, Throckmorton, and Manners curtsy.*

ELIZABETH [*over her shoulder*]. Sir Walter will not. [*The others start.*] I have recalled him to Court. [*Turning again*] But hardly he won my consent to his going, and since he left London I have bethought myself that he shall not be wasted as Sidney was. There are adventurers a-plenty to pluck the golden apples o' the Spanish Main, but only one Raleigh. We need him here.

[*Elizabeth and Radcliffe go off. They do not see that Throckmorton, terrified, has risen from her curtsy and is standing rigid, staring after them. Howard and Manners rise. Elizabeth has left her fan on the chair.*

MANNERS [*anxiously*]. Why, Mistress Throckmorton, what is the matter? Are you ill?

HOWARD [*lightly*]. 'Slife, Bess! What ails you? Sir Walter is coming back to Court, and you stand looking like a—like—[*at a loss*] what does she look like, Bridget?

MANNERS [*catching Howard's arm*]. S'sh, Mary!

HOWARD [*ignoring her, teasing Throckmorton*]. I know what 'tis! Sir Walter is coming back, but at the *Queen's* command. [*Laughing*] A woman needs must be queen in her particular man's heart, and will have no rival there, though that rival be a queen indeed and great as Gloriana. Aha, Mistress Elizabeth Throckmorton! Two Elizabeths in one man's heart are a crowd, methinks. Are your eyes *green*, Bess?

THROCKMORTON [*breaking her spell of horror and turning on Howard, passionately*]. A God's mercy end your mocking! I pray you be never in my strait. [*Whispering in an agony of fear*] What shall we do—now? Oh, kind God, what shall we do?

MANNERS. Bess—is there anything we may——

THROCKMORTON [*interrupting, walking up and down*]. I know her jealousy. I let him go, gladly, thinking he would be well away at sea before—before she must know that he and I are lovers. love each other

MANNERS [*aghast*]. Lovers!

HOWARD. Bess, you little fool!

THROCKMORTON [*ignoring this*]. He'd have made a great voyage. I know he would, for he is greater than all of them. And, by the time he had come home again, she'd have found a new fancy, and would mind him only for the treasure he brought back to her grasp.

HOWARD. But what about you?

THROCKMORTON. It—does not matter about me.

HOWARD. Does it not? You wait until her Grace gets word o' this. Raleigh is no man to leave you thus to face her alone.

THROCKMORTON [*quietly*]. He did not know that our love must needs be discovered. . . . And he was full of his dreams o' the west; the wonders to be seen; the new lands to be found and claimed for England; all the new world growing up across those weeks of ocean . . . [*Gently*] A woman does not stand between a man and his dreams.

HOWARD. You may tell the Queen that, though I doubt if 'twill keep her nails from your face. Of all the utter folly! Surely there is warning enough in the history o' this place? You know how she was when Leicester married secretly. You remember the doleful tale of milady Catherine Grey.

THROCKMORTON. But Catherine Grey was heir to the throne. That was why she might not marry without the Queen's permission——

HOWARD. Raleigh is the Queen's favourite, and you'll find this matter will be no lighter than the other. She is old, and she grips hard at what she has. Leicester is dead, and Essex— [*with a mischievous smile*] Essex dances not yet to *her* tune. Think you that she will let Raleigh go—and to you? [*Pause, Throckmorton increasingly dismayed.*] She'll raise a greater clamour than the Tower lions at feeding-time; a storm to destroy another armada. Raleigh may temper it to himself by jilting you——

THROCKMORTON [*hotly*]. He never would——

HOWARD. I'm none so sure o' that. But, however 'tis, there's no escape for you, Bess. 'Sdeath! I'd not be in your shoes for a thousand pounds.

THROCKMORTON. She has commanded him back, and—oh God! what will happen to him when she knows——

[*Throckmorton drops into the chair and bursts into tears. Howard and Manners go up to her.*

MANNERS. You think only of him, but 'tis of yourself you must think. We must make a plan for you——

HOWARD. Bess—I'm sorry I tormented you. I did not know—— [*Radcliffe enters.*

RADCLIFFE. Her Grace's fan—she left it on the chair. [*Starting as she sees the others*] Why, what's amiss here?

HOWARD [*quickly*]. Bess is not well this morning.

RADCLIFFE. She must indeed be ill to weep of it. I know her, and I've never known her weep for her own sickness. What's amiss, I say?

MANNERS. Nothing, good Mistress Radcliffe. That is— only a headache——

RADCLIFFE [*dryly*]. You've not been at Court long enough to learn to tell lies like truths, milady Bridget. Moreover, I asked Mistress Bess here——

THROCKMORTON [*drying her eyes*]. 'Tis nothing. I was being silly——

HOWARD [*lightly, trying to ease the situation*]. As every woman on occasion is allowed to be.

RADCLIFFE [*curtly, to Howard*]. You seek too many such occasions. [*Pause, then Radcliffe adds pointedly*] Is this matter to do with Sir Walter Raleigh?

HOWARD [*innocently*]. Sir Walter Raleigh?

RADCLIFFE [*gesturing Howard to silence*]. Answer me, Bess.

I've not been altogether easy about you of late. Are you in love with Raleigh?

THROCKMORTON. Yes.

RADCLIFFE. And he with you?

THROCKMORTON [*after hesitation*]. Yes.

RADCLIFFE. Here's a pretty kettle o' fish! Will you maids never learn sense? I'd thought that you, Bess, at least—— [*Breaking off, patting Throckmorton's shoulder, kindly*] There, there! Take it not hardly. You are not generally given to follies, child, and you will forget this. [*Pause. Radcliffe continues anxiously*] You know her Grace takes not kindly to love-affairs.

HOWARD. Except her own.

RADCLIFFE [*sharply, to Howard*]. Peace, impudence! [*To Throckmorton*] You know, too, that Sir Walter is much in the Queen's favour.

THROCKMORTON [*passionately*]. Must she have all? Are we no more than slaves that we may not make our lives for ourselves?

RADCLIFFE [*surprised*]. How now? Rebellion—from you? Why, 'tis most unlike you! I'm an old woman, child, ay! and an old maid too. I can tell you this: there's no man on earth worth wasting a tear for. Our mistress is worth the whole pack o' them ten times over.

[*Pause. Growing tension. Radcliffe becomes more uneasy.*] How far has this matter gone between you and Raleigh?

[*Pause.*

HOWARD [*impulsively*]. She will have to know, Bess. [*To Radcliffe*] Mistress Radcliffe—you may have anything o' the Queen. Use your good offices to gain leave for Bess to—to go home to the country for a while.

[*Throckmorton has drooped. Radcliffe looks at her, aghast.*

RADCLIFFE. God-a-mercy! That women can be such fools! . . . The Queen must be told o' this.

THROCKMORTON [*desperately*]. No!

HOWARD. She bears grudges. She'll never forgive Bess——

THROCKMORTON. Oh, it matters not about me! 'Tis for him I fear. Sweet Mistress Radcliffe, she must not be told——

RADCLIFFE. There is no remedy. You do not know her as I know. She learns of everything—everything—and it goes hard with any who try to keep the truth from her. She's not changed in these matters—except for the worse—since, half a lifetime ago, she sent Catherine Grey to the Tower.

[*Pause. Then, in the silence, Elizabeth's voice is heard, off, calling.*

ELIZABETH. Radcliffe! [*Pause, then impatiently*] Radcliffe!

RADCLIFFE [*hastily*]. She is impatient o' my absence.

ELIZABETH [*nearer*]. Mary! Where tarry you?

RADCLIFFE [*urgently*]. She's coming here! Compose yourself, Bess, for the love o' God, while we have time to think on this coil.

[*Hastily takes the fan, and is hurrying off when Elizabeth meets her in the doorway. Elizabeth is a little impatient, but still good-humoured.*

ELIZABETH. Why, Mary, you are as slow as a coach. The fan was in the chair, here, as I said?

RADCLIFFE [*backing, keeping between Elizabeth and Throckmorton*]. Yes, madam.

ELIZABETH. Then why, woman, do you choose to keep me waiting? Marry come up! Must I run my own errands?

RADCLIFFE. Your pardon! I was—directing the maids in a matter of some difficulty in the embroidery here.

ELIZABETH. So! The Queen of England must kick her heels while you turn sewing-mistress to a pack o' lazy hoydens? The world grows no better as we grow older.

RADCLIFFE. The world has ever fallen short of perfection, madam.

ELIZABETH [*laughing, snatching the opportunity to make a*

speech]. Ay, to be sure it has. You maids may well take that to heart, so that when you dream your dreams o' youthful follies you may know they are but dreams. If you would conquer life, and the world, you must learn—as I ha' done— to stand alone, the more especially to stand free from men. Love is the greatest delusion of all you suffer—eh, Mary? We'll have no maudlin love-affairs about us here—mark that! [*Manners and Howard recoil in astonishment, but Elizabeth does not see them.*] The world knows that I set ye a fair example. [*And she really believes what she says.*] You shall be sworn to Diana as I am, for virginity is a state most blessed. Confirm me, Mary.

[*Radcliffe has now backed to before Throckmorton, who is making great efforts to control herself.*

RADCLIFFE. Your Grace indeed speaks truth. I'd not change my state for the paragon of all mankind [*dryly*] whom no woman has ever met.

ELIZABETH [*laughing*]. Nor ever will.

HOWARD [*impulsively*]. Yet, madam, there are men about you of whom your Grace must be proud——

ELIZABETH. They are well enough, some of them, because they serve me. But their advantage is in statesmanship, in poetry, in war, in the sailing o' ships about the seas o' the world. [*Becoming a little annoyed*] Not one o' them was ever the better for love. And, while my memory is on you, I'd tell you this, Howard: your dresses are too fine for a maid o' your years.

HOWARD [*as catty as she dare be*]. But youth, surely, is the time for pretty dresses.

ELIZABETH [*harshly*]. So you'd teach me, ha? I say that you draw undue attention t' your person, which is immodest and unbecoming.

HOWARD. Your pardon, madam, but—I am not immodest.

ELIZABETH [*angrily*]. You'd be opposite with me? You shall know that I am not to be outfaced by a brat o' your years and in my privy chamber. [*Moving about impatiently*] Is't not enough that I must for ever be arguing with my Council? [*Half to herself*] They will not grant this—they must ever demand that! I must marry, forsooth! Or, being unwed, I must name an heir—as though I'd spend my days in sight o' my winding-sheet. [*Suddenly*] Where is my fan, Mary? [*With a note of girlish excitement*] We must go choose my dress. Raleigh will be here anon, and he has a keen eye for such matters.

> [*Radcliffe gives Elizabeth the fan. As she does so she moves away from Throckmorton, whom Elizabeth notices.*]

What, tears here? And wherefore have you been howling? Come, girl, out with it!

THROCKMORTON. I crave your Grace's pardon—I am indisposed.

ELIZABETH. Indisposed—ha? Too much marchpane and sugar-meat, belike. Get yourself a draught for the blood.

THROCKMORTON. Yes, madam.

ELIZABETH. I had thirty years ere you had one, and do you see me mumping with headaches and megrims? I can ride all day and dance all night wi' the best o' you youngsters, and be fresh at my prayers every dawn.

RADCLIFFE. But your Grace sets a hard standard for ordinary mortals.

ELIZABETH [*laughing heartily, clapping Radcliffe on the shoulder, with something of her father's manner*]. Marry, and that do I! My father took life heartily, and I am his very daughter. He woke our England to richness and laughter, and I will keep her so awake. [*Viciously*] There will be no mumbling Papist James, nor any other, to lord it here in my place for many a year yet. . . . [*Staring at Throckmorton, changing her manner*] What is the matter with that wench? 'Tis somewhat more than a megrim. She is white as a new corpse. [*Sharply*] What ails the girl? [*Aside, fearfully, to Radcliffe*] Know you of any cases o' the plague?

RADCLIFFE. Nay, nay, your Grace! She has not the plague. They look not so. 'Tis but a mere——

[*Throckmorton, whose effort to control herself has been too much for her, slips to the floor, fainting. Radcliffe and Howard run to her, raising her head on cushions. Howard holds a pomander under her nose. Radcliffe chafes her hands.*]

ELIZABETH [*dryly*]. A mere—something, I think. [*Anxiously*] You can be sure 'tis not the plague, Mary?

RADCLIFFE [*unhappily*]. Certain, madam. [*Trying to take advantage of the opportunity*] The maid has been ailing these last weeks. If your Grace would allow her to visit her home for a while——

ELIZABETH [*impatiently*]. Enough of it! Faugh! I'll have no puling ninnies about me. She must be made of better stuff than to run home to her father with every bellyache. Had she my burden to carry, then there might be some reason for it— but where might I turn had I the need?

RADCLIFFE [*persisting*]. Nevertheless, I feel that the country air would do her good——

ELIZABETH [*suspiciously*]. Methinks I've heard before, and not long since, that Mistress Bess here desires a sojourn in country air. . . . Why?

[*Throckmorton, who has revived, struggles to sit up. The others, under Elizabeth's rapidly growing suspicion and anger, are increasingly uneasy.*]

Perchance she grows weary o' the Court, and of us? We are too dull and dowdy for her, is that it?

THROCKMORTON [*faintly*]. No, your Grace——

ELIZABETH. Have I not said that we go on progress in the country? And would you refuse to attend the Queen so that you might go home and attend your father's chickens, wench?

RADCLIFFE. Please, madam—the maid is ill.

ELIZABETH. And of what? Of what?

[*Pause. Throckmorton struggles to her feet, her extreme despair giving her courage and dignity.*]

THROCKMORTON. Madam, I have served you well, I hope —but I am no more than any other, and there are many who would be—honoured to take my place. I—I crave your Grace's permission to withdraw from the Court.

[*Pause. Elizabeth grasps Throckmorton's meaning.*

ELIZABETH. So! ... [*Quietly, over a dawning fury*] And what has Sir Nicholas, your father, to say to this?

THROCKMORTON. He does not know.

ELIZABETH [*rapidly*]. He does not know! A pretty coil, in sooth! And what, think you, is to be the reputation o' my Court, if wenches are to come here only to be sent home in disgrace? Have you thought o' that—ha? Living here with me, you are under the care o' the head o' the Church, and must so behave. Have you considered of that? What are my people to say o' my Court? What are the Papists to mumble into Romish ears at their secret meetings—ha? Is that Italian woman o' the Medici to cackle over me, or pious Philip to roll up his eyes in holy horror o' the back-slidings of a decadent English Court—ha?

[*Elizabeth has worked herself into a fury. Now she pauses to spit a more personal question.*]

Who is y'r lover, girl?

[*Tense pause. Elizabeth strides to Throckmorton.*]

You hear me? Who is y'r lover?

THROCKMORTON [*quietly*]. He is known to none but myself, madam.

ELIZABETH. What? Some varlet o' the streets, saucy merchant, apprentice, or strolling player? Think you that I ha' lost all my wits? He is *of the Court*, and you shall tell me his name.

[*As Throckmorton is silent, Elizabeth, now fearful as well as angry, grips her shoulders, shaking her.*]

Tell me his name!

THROCKMORTON. Oh, madam, the fault is mine! He shall not be blamed——

ELIZABETH. Who?

THROCKMORTON. I'll not tell you—unless I have your promise you'll not harm him.

ELIZABETH. You make conditions with me? Are you so besotted as to forget to whom you speak? Who is he?

THROCKMORTON [*obstinately*]. You'll not punish him?

ELIZABETH [*furiously*]. I'll—— [*Controlling herself, becoming crafty, desperately anxious to know that her growing fears are unfounded*] Well, I shall have no interest in punishing the man. 'Tis you fools of doting girls who are ever to blame. But I must know—— [*Brief pause.*

THROCKMORTON. Sir Walter Raleigh.

[*Elizabeth's fears are realized. She puts her hands to her mouth and backs away from Throckmorton, staring at her, seeing in her youth the mockery of her own age. As she backs across the room and stands near the table she is a trembling old woman. Tense pause, attention of all directed on Elizabeth, who controls her trembling, draws herself erect, rigid, flashing anger, then, her fury gaining on her, sweeps her hand viciously across the chessmen, scattering them in all directions.*

RADCLIFFE [*taking a step towards her*]. Ah—madam——

[*Elizabeth brushes her aside, going to her chair and sinking into it. Her mask of anger slowly breaks up, and she bursts into tears.*

ELIZABETH. *Raleigh!* . . . And he could not be faithful. Is there no man can be faithful to me? Oh, am I to be lonely all my days—withered—frustrated—I who had the pick of all the princes o' Christendom? . . . Leicester deceived me, too. . . . Alençon was driven away. . . . Essex is rude as the north wind. And now—my gentle Raleigh. He spoke me fair and—and I—oh God! what fools we women can be to trust in the words of men——

RADCLIFFE [*indicating the others*]. Madam—hush!

ELIZABETH [*hardening*]. Nay, but I will speak my heart out. 'Sdeath! I'll not stop at words, neither! [*Springing up, striding to Throckmorton, viciously slapping her face, then taking her by the shoulders and shaking her*] ~~You little strumpet!~~ You'd dare triumph over a queen, would you? I'll have you in a dungeon for this, ay! and your lover to the block——

[*Throckmorton screams.*

RADCLIFFE.
HOWARD.   } Madam!
MANNERS.

THROCKMORTON. But, your Grace—your promise! You said he'd not be hurt——

ELIZABETH [*grimly*]. *He* said a-many things—then turned from me to you. From me—to *you*! [*Throwing Throckmorton aside*] Enough of it! You'll t' the Tower—the pair o' ye.

[*Throckmorton crouches in despair. Elizabeth stands, pant-ing, in a royal rage now. The others watch her. Knocking, off. For a moment this goes unnoticed, then Manners hears it and steals off, to return almost immediately, whispering to Radcliffe.*

RADCLIFFE. Madam—Milord Burghley craves your ear. [*Pause, Elizabeth unheeding.*] There is a matter of grave importance—a matter of state, madam.

ELIZABETH. Eh?

RADCLIFFE. Milord Burghley—a matter of state——

ELIZABETH [*pulling herself together, putting her hands to her head, wearily*]. Burghley—for ever Burghley and matters of state. . . . Well, I must see to him.

[*Elizabeth draws herself up, turns, and goes off slowly, the others, except Throckmorton, curtsying.*

CURTAIN

DAUGHTERS OF INVENTION

A COMEDY

by Nora Ratcliff

CHARACTERS

MRS TRUBY-TAIT
ANGELA } *her daughters*
NELLIE
MISS FEATHERGILL, *poor relation–cum–secretary*
FLOSSIE, *family retainer*
MISS JAMIESON, *journalist*

SCENE: A sitting-room
TIME: The present

DAUGHTERS OF INVENTION

SCENE: *A pleasant lounge in a middle-class home. A window at the back stretches across about three-quarters of the stage. The cretonne curtains are of a strikingly original design, and so are the furniture coverings. There is a settee L.C., with rather violent-coloured cushions. An armchair is a little down-stage, to the right; a writing-table down-stage L., with chair; a pouffe between the settee and the footlights. A door up-stage on the right wall leads to the hall; half way down, on the opposite side, is a door to an adjoining room. It is a bright afternoon in spring.*

Before the curtain rises we hear a scale being sung—not too skilfully. Slowly and carefully each note is sounded and held. The curtain rises. Angela, the vocalist (about 23 years old), is standing in the centre of the stage. Seated on the pouffe at her feet is Nellie (about 17); she is gazing admiringly up at her sister. After about three more notes Angela has finished the scale and pauses.

NELLIE. You know, I think you ought to try now and see how long you can hold one single note—La-a-ah—like that. I'll time you. Wait till I say "Go." [*She examines her wrist watch in readiness.*] Now.

ANGELA [*after a deep breath*]. La-a-ah . . .

    [*The end of the note is rather quavering and breathless.*
NELLIE. Mm. Twenty seconds. Try again. [*Angela tries again.*] Twenty-five. That's better. Now try and hold on for thirty.

    [*Angela tries again. Nellie keeps her eyes on the watch.*]
NELLIE [*as Angela shows signs of weakening*]. Twenty-six, twenty-seven. . . . Hang on, Angela—— [*Angela stops and gasps for breath.*] Twenty-eight and a half. What on earth did you stop for?

ANGELA. Breath.

NELLIE. Well, go on again now. Try a lower note. Perhaps that'll help.

ANGELA. La-a-a-ah . . .

NELLIE. Twenty-eight . . . twenty-nine . . . thirty! [*She jumps up and hugs her sister delightedly.*] Darling, that's marvellous! Superb! One of these days you'll be a really great singer, and then you'll remember how I helped you, won't you, darling? You know, it's as good as being famous yourself, to know that you've helped to make somebody else famous. I shall come to your concerts and listen to you, and think of how I've sat here, day after day——

ANGELA. But you haven't. This is the first day.

NELLIE. Of course it is. The first of hundreds of times. Come on. See if you can do it again.

ANGELA. La . . . [*She stops suddenly.*] Oh, Nellie, there's one thing I'm not sure of. I wonder if you can look right down my throat when I'm singing. See if I manage to tuck away the little thing that hangs down at the back of my mouth, a pink waggly thing . . . like that.

[*She illustrates by hanging her hand from the wrist and waggling her index finger.*

NELLIE. All right, come a bit nearer. [*Angela moves nearer to the pouffe. Nellie mounts on it and prepares to peer down her sister's throat.*] Better try a scale first. [*Angela does so.*] O.K. That's fine. Now, one note.

ANGELA [*after a deep breath*]. M-m-m-ah.

NELLIE [*in the manner of a boxing referee, lowering the hand at each count*]. Ten, fifteen, twenty . . .

[*Enter Miss Feathergill. She is a 'poor relation' of Mrs Truby-Tait's and her self-appointed secretary and general runabout. She carries a few papers and magazines and over her arm is a shallow gardening basket that holds more papers, knitting, and heaven knows what.*

MISS FEATHERGILL [*pausing at the door*]. What on earth . . .

NELLIE. Damn!

MISS FEATHERGILL. Nellie, please!

NELLIE. Well, it's too bad. She'd made twenty-eight and the little thingamijig was tucked away ever so beautifully.

MISS FEATHERGILL. What on earth are you talking about? And I'm sure your poor dear mother has enough to put up with without your making this terrible noise. Yes, indeed she has. Really, Angela, the place sounded like a zoo.

NELLIE. I guess it was Mother who thought of that one. And it just isn't true. Angela was singing beautifully. It's not fair to discourage genius.

MISS FEATHERGILL. Don't be absurd, Nellie. And you'd better get off that pouffe before your mother sees you standing on the new cretonne.   [Nellie jumps down.

ANGELA. Is Mother coming down here?

MISS FEATHERGILL [fussing over to the writing-table]. Of course. You know she always receives people here. Now, where did I put the proofs of that last article for Home Hints?

[The basket tips up and scatters papers, etc. She kneels on the floor to retrieve them.

NELLIE. Why, who is she receiving? And how's she going to get down here with a sprained ankle?

MISS FEATHERGILL. Your mother is a strong-minded woman and she isn't likely to let a little thing like that upset her appointments.

NELLIE. She doesn't mind upsetting Angela's practice, though.

MISS FEATHERGILL. Ah, here they are—yes, indeed.

[She finds the proofs and stands up. Angela strolls across to look at them over Miss Feathergill's shoulder.

ANGELA. What's it about this time?

MISS FEATHERGILL. The patent new draught-preventer that your mother invented last week.

NELLIE. Not that crack-brained contraption she fell over

when she twisted her ankle? Is it fair to go risking other people's lives like that?

MISS FEATHERGILL. The fact that your mother forgot it was there and fell over it doesn't mean that it wasn't a success as a draught-obstructor.

ANGELA. Well, it isn't much of a recommendation, is it?

MISS FEATHERGILL. These little accidents are bound to occur now and again.

NELLIE. Now and again! I like that. It's not three months since Mother smashed her wrist with the patent coal-breaker . . .

MISS FEATHERGILL. She sold the patent for one hundred pounds.

ANGELA. To the Bone-setters' Guild, no doubt.

NELLIE. And six weeks ago she singed half her hair off playing about with a safety device on the dryer.

MISS FEATHERGILL. The Hairdressers' Association gave her a special certificate for that.

NELLIE. They ought to have given her a wig.

ANGELA [reading the proofs over Miss Feathergill's shoulder]. Seriously, I don't think Mother ought to let that go to print without adding a word of warning that short-sighted people ought not to use it.

NELLIE. If you ask me, Mother's a public menace.

MISS FEATHERGILL. In the last issue of Home Hints the Editress said that your mother had done more to smooth the path of the over-worked housewife than any other single person in the country.

NELLIE. Well, I'd say she made housework a positive obstacle race. Ask poor Flossie.

MISS FEATHERGILL. Flossie is getting very difficult nowadays. As your mother told her the other day, she is hopelessly old-fashioned and has no imagination. Now where's that letter from the Secretary of the Work-Shy Housewives' Association? [She flurries about among the papers.

E

ANGELA [*bored; setting to work with a nail file*]. Who's coming this afternoon, Feathers?

MISS FEATHERGILL. Miss Jamieson of the *Medborough Herald* has an appointment for three o'clock.

ANGELA. Miss Jamieson? Why, that's A.K.J. who does the music and concert reviews. What's she want to see Mum for?

MISS FEATHERGILL. She's the Editor's daughter and does the weekly Woman's Page as well. She's writing up your mother in her special series of *Famous Women of our County*.

NELLIE. I should think that by now Mum's notorious, never mind famous.

MISS FEATHERGILL. That's most disrespectful of you, Nellie. Yes, indeed, most disrespectful. Your mother has——

NELLIE *and* ANGELA. —done more to lighten the load of the housewife——

[*Enter Flossie, the housekeeper. She is tall, gaunt, and big-boned; a Yorkshirewoman (or any suitable dialect speaker). She is holding her left wrist, round which she has twisted a handkerchief that is already blood-stained.*

FLOSSIE [*indignantly*]. 'Ere, just see what yon daft safety-knife has done!

NELLIE. Oh, poor Flossie! Let me——

FLOSSIE. I'll manage it meself, thanks, Miss Nellie. But I've come to tell your mother 'at I'm not going to use the thing no more. Straight at t'back o' t'fire it's gone.

MISS FEATHERGILL. Oh, but Flossie——

FLOSSIE. That thing isn't going to be used again i' my kitchen, I tell you straight. Not if she goes down on her bended knees it isn't. Young Alice slashed herself wi' it yesterday, and now I've nigh chopped me hand off.

MISS FEATHERGILL. Are you sure, Flossie, that you and Alice have been using it the right way? Did you use it exactly as Mrs Truby-Tait showed you?

FLOSSIE. The way she showed us it 'ud 'ave taken three or four days to do enough pertaties for one meal. If she thinks a busy woman can go finicking around wi' her patent this and her patent that, wi' a family of six to cook for——

MISS FEATHERGILL. But *Home Hints* said——

FLOSSIE. I don't care what *'Ome 'Ints* said or didn't say. It's what I have to say 'at matters. Last week I slid downstairs on one of her patent non-skid mats. If I was to show you them bruises——

MISS FEATHERGILL. Thank you, but we——

FLOSSIE. It's a miracle I didn't break my back. I tell you, if this is going on much longer I'm giving in me notice. It isn't safe, living in a place like this, more like a lunatic asylum than a decent house. What she wants to go on wi' this labour-saving stuff for I can't make out. It isn't as if she ever did a 'and's turn in t'place 'ersen——

MISS FEATHERGILL. Flossie, I really can't allow you to speak like that of your mistress.

FLOSSIE. Well, she should leave us alone and let us do t'work our own road. When yer pay folk to do a job yer should trust 'em to do it, and not go cluttering 'em up wi' this and that.

ANGELA. You'd better peel the potatoes your own way, Flossie. Mother'll never know if you don't say anything about it.

MISS FEATHERGILL. Now, run along, Flossie. I'll come and find you some bandaging.

FLOSSIE. I know where t'First Aid stuff is. If I didn't, some on us 'ud a bled to death i' this daft house long sin'.

MISS FEATHERGILL [*as Flossie turns to go*]. Oh—and Flossie, Mrs Truby-Tait is expecting a visitor at three o'clock, a Miss Jamieson. Show her straight in here, please, and if anyone else calls, your mistress is not at home.

FLOSSIE [*muttering as she goes out*]. T'way things is going on there'll soon be no 'ome to be h'at. [*Exit.*

MISS FEATHERGILL. Really, that woman is becoming quite impossible.

NELLIE. I think Flossie is just grand.

ANGELA. A bit crude, perhaps. I say, Feathers, what line is Mum taking with Miss Jamieson? Do we get our knitting and tatting, and stage the domesticated Mother and Daughters show? Or is it one of her "lonely mother turns to other interests" interviews?

MISS FEATHERGILL. Your mother said it was a very important interview. She hopes to make some useful contacts through Miss Jamieson's father. She said she wanted you both to keep out of the way.

ANGELA. Hm. I thought it would happen like that, just when somebody really interesting comes along. I'd like to meet Miss Jamieson, and then we could talk about music. She might have some free tickets for concerts.

MISS FEATHERGILL. Your mother said she wanted to see Miss Jamieson *alone*. Oh, Nellie, would you mind tidying those papers? I must go and help your mother downstairs. Angela, perhaps you would make the settee comfortable.

[*Miss Feathergill goes out. The girls carry on with their tasks in not too good a humour.*

ANGELA [*as she shakes and arranges the cushions*]. I'd like to scatter the settee with drawing pins!

NELLIE. I think it's a bit mean of Mother, not to give you a chance of meeting Miss Jamieson.

ANGELA. You know what Mother is.

NELLIE. Do I know! Angela, I think we ought to put our foot down.

ANGELA. What do you mean?

NELLIE. Flossie was right.

ANGELA. How 'right'?

NELLIE. If this sort of thing goes on there soon won't be a "'ome' to be h'at." One of these fine days Mother will kill either herself or somebody else.

ANGELA. Or somebody will kill Mother. Oh, I don't know; it's just as likely she'll really invent something by accident—and then she'll be famous.

NELLIE. And what difference will that make to us? She'll be so busy being famous she won't have time to bother about us at all. Of course, I don't mind much. I've no ambitions yet. But there's your singing.

ANGELA. That's why I wanted to meet Miss Jamieson. She's bound to know people who matter.

NELLIE. Angela, I've got an idea. I think we can really teach Mother a lesson.

ANGELA. What do you mean?

NELLIE. Never mind. Do as I tell you. . . . Where's that patent afternoon-tea tray?

ANGELA. But it doesn't work properly.

NELLIE. I know it doesn't, my precious. Take it to Flossie and tell her that Mother particularly wants tea serving on it——

ANGELA. But——

NELLIE. Please, darling, do as I say. Remember—all great artists have a manager—somebody who looks after them and boosts them—like on the pictures. Well, I'm going to be yours. [*Thrusting the tray into Angela's hands and pushing her out to the hall*] Here, take it. And then come through to me in the other room. Then I'll tell you the really exciting part of my plan.

> [*She pushes Angela out and then stands, surveying the room, like a general on a prospective battlefield. Enter Mrs Truby-Tait, supporting herself with a walking-stick. Miss Feather-gill is helping her on the other side. Mrs Truby-Tait is an imposing specimen of womanhood, dressed in an elaborate restgown, a sort of turban wound round her head to hide the ravages of the patent dryer. She stands a little way in from the door, and, in her turn, surveys the scene.*]

MRS TRUBY-TAIT [*pointing with her stick*]. Nellie, the pouffe, please—over there. [*She directs Nellie to an appropriate position.*] M—yes. . . . That's better. Now, the armchair, dear, turned just a *leetle* . . . No, no, you stupid child! [*Nellie grimaces and turns it the other way.*] Of course. Do you think I want to talk to the woman's back? And now run along, darling. I don't want to be disturbed.

NELLIE. Mum, don't you think it would be a good idea to let Angela——

MRS TRUBY-TAIT. The only good idea I can think of at the moment, darling, is that you should leave me here undisturbed.

NELLIE [*gallantly making another effort*]. Mum, I've been thinking——

[*Mrs Truby-Tait goes off into a peal of tinkling laughter.*

MRS TRUBY-TAIT. My darling, I'm sure you have. And perhaps later on, when Mummy isn't busy, her little Nellie shall tell Mummy what it's all about.

NELLIE. For heaven's sake, Mother, will you never stop talking as if you and me were two other people?

MRS TRUBY-TAIT. You and I, darling. And don't start being whimsical, you funny child. [*She moves carefully over to the settee.*] Run along now, darling.

NELLIE. Oh . . . damn!   [*She flounces out, L.*

MISS FEATHERGILL. I do wish you'd speak to Nellie about her language, Mrs T.T. That's the word she used when I came in here a little while ago. Oh, and Flossie, too. She's been most impertinent. Yes, indeed. Most imp——

MRS TRUBY-TAIT. My dear Feathers, I just can't have you worrying me with domestic tittle-tattle just at present. This interview——

MISS FEATHERGILL [*a little hurt*]. If you call a threatened revolution among the domestic staff mere tittle-tattle, of course I've nothing more to say. Nothing more at all. And that's what it is—revolution. Nothing more and nothing less.

MRS TRUBY-TAIT. My dear Feathers, you're an alarmist, and, like all alarmists, you shriek for extreme measures before they're necessary. You encourage Flossie to chatter. If she is impertinent send her out of the room and have done with it.

MISS FEATHERGILL. She threatened to give notice.

MRS TRUBY-TAIT. That's just the point. She can't threaten to give notice if she isn't in the room, can she? Use your common sense, woman.

[*Re-enter Angela.*

Well, what do you want, Angela? I hope you've finished that dreadful bawling and screaming you were indulging in a few minutes ago.

ANGELA. Really, Mother, I was only——

MRS TRUBY-TAIT. There, there, child. I'm not scolding. We must all have our hobbies, I suppose. But I must admit that there are times when I wish yours was drawing—or keeping rabbits.

ANGELA [*as she crosses to the door, L.*]. You ought to be damned thankful that it isn't bagpipes. [*She bangs the door behind her.*

MISS FEATHERGILL [*reacting in horror*]. Oh, dear! What has got into the girls to-day?

MRS TRUBY-TAIT. Perhaps it's the weather. I used to give them brimstone and treacle at this time of the year when they were little children. [*The doorbell rings, off-stage.*] My notes, Feathers.

[*Miss Feathergill fusses over to the writing-table; returns with a small writing-pad. Arranges the restgown and smooths the rug over Mrs Truby-Tait's feet.*

[*Enter Flossie, announcing Miss Jamieson.*

FLOSSIE. Miss Jamieson. [*Exit.*

[*Miss Jamieson is a brisk young person, 25 or 26 years old. A small black hat is balanced jauntily at the side of her head. She affects the semi-masculine in her clothes: a dark, severely cut suit, relieved by a frilly white blouse; dainty shoes and fine silk stockings. Horn-rimmed glasses; a direct manner.*

MISS JAMIESON. Good afternoon, Mrs Truby-Tait. [*She has no hesitation as to which of the two women is her victim.*] It's very good of you to see me. I hope I'm not——

MRS TRUBY-TAIT. Not at all, not at all. You'll forgive my not rising, but a slight accident to my ankle——

MISS JAMIESON. But how very unfortunate! Not too serious, I hope? You're sure I'm not disturbing you?

MRS TRUBY-TAIT. By no means. Allow me to introduce my friend, Miss Feathergill. [*The women shake hands, murmuring appropriately.*] Please——

[*Mrs Truby-Tait waves to the armchair. Miss Jamieson sits.*

MISS JAMIESON. So at last I've bearded the lioness in her den. The ankle isn't going to hinder your work too badly, I hope. Must be very annoying for a busy woman like yourself——

MRS TRUBY-TAIT [*making use of the silvery laugh*]. Oh, dear me, no! We can't allow little mishaps like this to interfere with our work, can we, Feathers? A sprained ankle, fortunately, does not prevent one from thinking.

MISS JAMIESON. So you work out all these clever inventions of yours in your head? But how amazing. Now, tell me, do you see the whole—er—idea at once, complete, or do you work it out slowly, step by step?

MRS TRUBY-TAIT. Really, you make my humble little ideas sound so important! How would you say the ideas came to me, Feathers?

MISS FEATHERGILL. You *dreamed* the patent door-scraper, didn't you?

MRS TRUBY-TAIT. Ye-yes. Oh, yes.

MISS JAMIESON. Ah, this is interesting. You dreamed you saw a patent door-scraper, and then woke up and remembered it. How thrilling!

MRS TRUBY-TAIT. Yes. Hm. I seemed to be floating about above my garden, in the way one so often is in dreams. Freud explains all that, of course. Then I saw the Rector coming up the path, and his boots were terribly muddy. I've never seen, *never seen* such boots. Funny it should have been the Rector; he's usually very particular. I can't for the life of me make out what the association was.

MISS FEATHERGILL [*leaning forward earnestly*]. I tell her it was the suggestion of purity. He's a bachelor, you know.

[Mrs Truby-Tait, noting Miss Jamieson's quickly suppressed smile, rewards the interruption with a freezing stare.

MRS TRUBY-TAIT. Well, just when I was about to scream out to him to wipe his boots before he came into my house, I saw him pause, look down to the side of the door, and there was *the most* fascinating scraper! I examined it most carefully—in my dream, of course—and the moment I woke up I made drawings.

MISS FEATHERGILL. She showed them to me when I took in her early morning tea. Yes, indeed, the drawings of the scraper!

MISS JAMIESON [*scribbling in her notebook*]. How very interesting. And you actually had one made? Of course it was a success?

MRS TRUBY-TAIT. Well—er——

MISS FEATHERGILL [*confidentially*]. Yes—and no. You see, the postman fell over it two days in succession. Then we had a note from the G.P.O. to say that if we didn't remove it they would have to refuse to deliver our letters. Of course, that doesn't mean that it wasn't a success as a door-scraper. Unfortunately, the Rector didn't call until after we'd removed it, so we couldn't try it on him.

MISS JAMIESON. What a pity!

MRS TRUBY-TAIT. Of course, usually it is *necessity* that is indeed the mother of invention. For example, I find that it takes, say, half an hour to peel the potatoes. I realize that this means that three and a half hours each week are being spent on the preparation of one vegetable. And that comes to—er—— *[She turns to Miss Feathergill.*

MISS FEATHERGILL. We worked it out as exactly one hundred and eighty-two hours, that is nearly a whole week in every year spent in peeling potatoes!

MRS TRUBY-TAIT. Obviously some economy could be effected here. So I set to work upon the idea of a patent potato peeler. The Editress of *Home Hints* said it was revolutionary.

MISS FEATHERGILL. And our housekeeper seems to agree with her.

MISS JAMIESON. You try all your inventions out at home, then? How very interesting that must be for your servants.

MRS TRUBY-TAIT [*with a grim look at Miss Feathergill, who is leaning forward as if about to speak*]. It is. Very.

MISS JAMIESON. And would it be indiscreet to ask what is your latest gift to the harassed housewife?

> [*Miss Feathergill hands Mrs Truby-Tait the proof sheet from the writing-table.*

MRS TRUBY-TAIT. I've just completed an original type of draught-excluder.

MISS JAMIESON. Very interesting. And you have tried it here? And it is successful?

MISS FEATHERGILL. Yes, indeed. Nothing can get past it.

> [*Mrs Truby-Tait glares at her and she shrinks back into silence.*

MRS TRUBY-TAIT. I've written an article about it for next week's *Home Hints*. You see, the great difficulty about excluding draughts is that you——

> [*From the next room comes the sound of a piano accompaniment and a soprano rendering of* The Lass with the Delicate Air. *After the first start of annoyance Mrs Truby-Tait continues her discourse.*]

The—er—the great difficulty is in deciding whether a door opens inward or—er—outward.

MISS JAMIESON [*who is listening to the music*]. Really——

MISS FEATHERGILL. Of course. That's *very* important.

MRS TRUBY-TAIT. You see, if a door opens *this* way, and the room is on this side—you follow?—then the pressure of the air will come—er—that is—the current of draught—er— Oh, Feathers, do please go and ask the girls not to make so much noise.

MISS JAMIESON [*who is interested*]. The girls? Your daughters?

MRS TRUBY-TAIT. Yes. Please go, Feathers. [*Miss Feathergill goes into the next room.*] I'm sorry we've been interrupted like this. I really don't know what they can be thinking of. Most distracting.

MISS JAMIESON. Not at all. We may be able to use this in the story. How old are they?

MRS TRUBY-TAIT. They're—well—they're growing up, you know, they're growing up.

MISS JAMIESON. You mean——

MRS TRUBY-TAIT. Amazing, isn't it, and a little sad, how quickly one's baby of yesterday becomes the child of to-day, and the child grows in years and understanding, and the young girl of to-day will become——

MISS JAMIESON. How many daughters have you, Mrs Truby-Tait?

MRS TRUBY-TAIT [*rather shortly*]. Two. And, as I was saying——

MISS JAMIESON. They're obviously interested in music. Now I——

[*Enter Nellie, followed by Miss Feathergill, who makes a helpless gesture in answer to Mrs Truby-Tait's frown of annoyance.*

NELLIE [*with an affectation of naïve spontaneity*]. Oh, Mum, darling, we're ever so sorry if we disturbed you. We forgot you were busy.

MRS TRUBY-TAIT. You know how much I dislike noise, and——

NELLIE. But you know what Angela is, Mummy. She can only practise when the mood seizes her——

MRS TRUBY-TAIT. Angela practise!

MISS FEATHERGILL. Oh, Nellie!

MRS TRUBY-TAIT. I told you, Nellie, that I wished——

NELLIE. Are you Miss Jamieson? The famous A.K.J.?

MISS JAMIESON. Well, I'm not sure about the 'famous,' but I am A.K.J. And you're Miss Truby-Tait—the elder or the younger?

NELLIE. Oh, the younger. Angela's twenty-three. She sings, you know. She's simply dying to meet you.

MISS JAMIESON. You don't mean that it was your sister singing just now? I thought——

NELLIE [*avoiding the lie direct*]. She works and works at her singing, but it's so difficult to get a chance nowadays. We thought, perhaps . . . She's dying to meet you, but she's rather shy.

MRS TRUBY-TAIT. Angela shy!

NELLIE [*smiling understandingly*]. I always think it's so difficult, don't you, Miss Jamieson, for a—well, a genius in her own right to understand her own daughters? And Mummy's so busy—aren't you, darling?—inventing practical, useful, everyday things, that she just hasn't time for art.

MRS TRUBY-TAIT. Nellie, this nonsense——

MISS JAMIESON. I'd very much like to meet your sister. If that was your sister's voice——

MRS TRUBY-TAIT. Miss Jamieson, I must——

MISS JAMIESON. I'm probably being very rude, Mrs Truby-Tait, but music's so much more in my line than household gadgets.

NELLIE [*turning back to the other room*]. I'll fetch Angela.

MRS TRUBY-TAIT. Miss Jamieson, before this goes any further——

MISS FEATHERGILL. Yes, indeed, Miss Jamieson, we ought——
[*Re-enter Nellie, followed by Angela.*

NELLIE. Here's my sister, Miss Jamieson.

MISS JAMIESON. How do you do, Miss Truby-Tait? Your sister has been saying——

ANGELA [*embarrassed, as she shakes hands*]. Good afternoon. I—er——

MRS TRUBY-TAIT. Once and for all, Nellie, this ridiculous joke of yours must stop. Miss Jamieson, we owe you a deep apology . . .

MISS JAMIESON. Not at all. I'm genuinely interested. [*To Angela*] Tell me about your singing.

ANGELA. Nellie, I'm so ashamed——

MISS FEATHERGILL. I should think you are, Angela. And Nellie would be even more ashamed, if she had any sense of shame at all.

NELLIE. Well, I'm sorry, but——

MISS JAMIESON. Don't bother to explain that that was only a gramophone record. I'm afraid I know that particular recording rather well. It's a favourite of mine.

NELLIE. You mean you knew——

MISS JAMIESON. Well, one can never be *quite* sure. It was a ruse to attract my attention, wasn't it? You succeeded very well. I'm sorry, Mrs Truby-Tait, but it was quite impossible to keep my mind fixed on draught-excluders when there was music within a few yards of me. You'll have to turn your attention to sound-proof doors.

MRS TRUBY-TAIT. I understood you were sent here by your father to interview me——

MISS JAMIESON. I was sent to collect a story about you and your home. It's the personal angle we want, you know.

MISS FEATHERGILL. My poor dear father always said that newspapers were most unscrupulous.

MISS JAMIESON. Miss Angela Truby-Tait has ambitions to become a singer, and her young sister is her devoted admirer. That's a good beginning.

NELLIE. I hope you're not just going to make a story out of it. It's help that Angela needs. I say, I've got an idea. Why shouldn't the *Medborough Herald* run a sort of competition for amateurs? You'd get lots of entries to cover expenses, and of course Angela would win. [*Solemnly*] There's lots of—of publicity value in the idea, isn't there?

MISS JAMIESON [*after looking at Nellie in silence for a moment, thinking it out*]. I believe you're right . . . I'll put the idea to Father as soon as I get home. Your daughter is as inventive as yourself, Mrs Truby-Tait.

MRS TRUBY-TAIT. I think both of my children have taken leave of their senses! You've never even heard Angela sing; yet you're willing to take her word for it that she is some neglected genius.

MISS JAMIESON. Whether she's a genius or not remains to be proved. But if she is, she won't be neglected long after Father has got to work on the Festival idea.

MRS TRUBY-TAIT [coldly]. Well, Miss Jamieson, if there's nothing else I can do for you, perhaps——

MISS JAMIESON. Please don't mistake my attitude to your own work, Mrs Truby-Tait. But, as a journalist, I'm bound to see, and I'm sure you'll understand, the immense story-value of your daughter's interests. I came here with a profound respect for your many useful inventions in the home, but our readers have always known quite a lot about that. It's the human side I was looking for—the reactions in the home of your work—the day-to-day life of a woman of genius——

[There is a heavy crash of crockery off-stage. A horrified pause. Flossie comes into the room and begins to speak the moment she is over the threshold, in spite of all Miss Feathergill's winks and nods to indicate that a stranger is present.

FLOSSIE. If you're expecting tea, I'm afraid ye'll be disappointed. If ye will go inventing daft contraptions 'at nobody in their senses would think of, ye've nobody but yerself to blame when they go wrong.

MRS TRUBY-TAIT. Flossie! What is the meaning of this?

FLOSSIE. Meaning? There's meaning and to spare. If ye'd come and take a look at the mess just outside t'kitchen door ye'd know well enough what I mean.

MRS TRUBY-TAIT. Will you tell me at once, Flossie, what has happened?

FLOSSIE. Your best tea set's i'smithereens, and t'cat's eating all t'sandwiches. And if ye want to blame owt ye can blame it on yer Truby-Tait patent serving-tray.

MRS TRUBY-TAIT. But I told you that wasn't to be used

any more. There were certain—er—certain adjustments to be made.

FLOSSIE. Well, I've just made 'em.

NELLIE. It was my fault, Mummy, not Flossie's. I thought it would be so nice if tea were served——

MISS FEATHERGILL. But, Nellie, surely you knew——

MRS TRUBY-TAIT. I'll deal with you later. What right had you to think at all, Miss Interference? It's a very good thing for you, Flossie, that I can't see the wreck you've made——

FLOSSIE. And why can't yer see it? Because you're lying there this very minute wi' an ankle ye smashed over another o' yer daft ideas. And here am I half crippled wi' yer stupid potato-peeler.

MISS FEATHERGILL. Flossie, please!

FLOSSIE. Ye can please away as 'ard as yer like. I've come here to give in me notice, once an' for all. I'm off to get a job where I'm not used as a dog to try it out on.

NELLIE. No, Flossie, please!

ANGELA. But, Flossie, what on earth's going to happen to us if you go? It won't be the same house without you.

FLOSSIE. Then ye'll have summat to be thankful for.

MISS FEATHERGILL ⎫   ⎧ Surely, Flossie, you won't
                   ⎪   ⎪   desert Mrs Truby-Tait at
                   ⎪   ⎪   such a time——

NELLIE   ⎬ [together] ⎨ Flossie, it was all my fault.
                   ⎪   ⎪   I never meant——

MRS TRUBY-TAIT   ⎪   ⎪ Of all the base ingratitude!
                   ⎪   ⎪   After the years you've been
                   ⎭   ⎩   in my house——

FLOSSIE [topping them all]. Will you shut up, all of yer! Such a pandemonium! An' a stranger 'ere an' all.

MRS TRUBY-TAIT. Flossie!

FLOSSIE [with real sincerity in her voice]. Mrs Truby-Tait, I've been i' this house for twenty-five years. For twenty of 'em you were a sane woman an' I was proud to be working for ye and helping wi' yer childer. And I'm as proud o' Miss Angela an' Miss Nellie there as if they were me own. But ever since ye invented that patent furniture polish—an' ye know as well as I do 'at that were only an accident through paraffin getting into t'salad cream—ever since then this house has been like a crazy place——

MRS TRUBY-TAIT. Flossie, how dare——

FLOSSIE. I'll dare a lot to bring you to yer senses. The nice creature ye were when ye first entered this house as a bride——

MRS TRUBY-TAIT. Flossie, I——

MISS FEATHERGILL. Before strangers——

FLOSSIE. It's a case of desperate remedies, Miss Feathergill. Now here's my—my ultimatun, as they say: either yer give me yer word, here and now, to drop this silly inventing business this very minute, or out of this house I walk, after twenty-five years o' service.

MISS FEATHERGILL. Flossie, do you realize what an outrageous suggestion——

FLOSSIE. Tell me any one thing ye've ever invented that's really worked.

MRS TRUBY-TAIT. There—there was the furniture polish.

FLOSSIE. Huh!

ANGELA. I really don't think you ought to talk to Mother like that, Flossie. . . .

MRS TRUBY-TAIT [sensing the dramatic possibilities]. No, no. Perhaps Flossie is right. I've tried to hide the truth from myself, but no—no—I must admit defeat. I should have realized that I have a duty to my children. . . . I have been too wrapped up in my career . . . [She begins to weep.] It is a bitter blow—a painful pill to swallow. [She gulps.] Flossie is right.   [She breaks down.

FLOSSIE. There's no need to start blubbering about it, ma'am. We've all had to put up wi' a lot o' nonsense, but I reckon, if you're coming to see reason——

MRS TRUBY-TAIT. Miss Jamieson, I have a message for your readers. It's very fortunate that you should have been here——

MISS JAMIESON. Most.

MRS TRUBY-TAIT. Tell them this—tell them . . .

MISS FEATHERGILL [*helpfully*]. "Nothing extenuate, nor set down aught in malice——"

MRS TRUBY-TAIT. Tell them that now my children are growing older they are needing much more of my time and attention. They are now at an age when a mother's comradeship and help—a mother's sympathy and understanding—is most needed. Their careers must be thought of. I must—with how much regret I leave it to your readers to imagine—give my time, my attention, and the modest ingenuity I happen to possess—I must give these up to my daughters. I must consecrate myself to their lives, submerge my interests in theirs. I must——

MISS JAMIESON. I've got the hang of it, I think. This will be a most interesting write-up.

MISS FEATHERGILL. Miss Jamieson, I do beg of you—you will . . .

MISS JAMIESON. Don't worry. I'm the soul of tact. And there's this Music Festival idea. I think we can work that in nicely. And if we can use Mrs Truby-Tait's name. . . .

MRS TRUBY-TAIT. Of course, of course. Haven't I said that all my interests are now centred upon my children?

FLOSSIE [*stolidly*]. And yer promise?

MRS TRUBY-TAIT. But haven't you just heard——

FLOSSIE. Ay, I've 'eard a lot o' rigmarole. But you'll still give me yer promise i' plain words.

NELLIE. I, Gwendoline Truby-Tait, do hereby solemnly declare——

FLOSSIE. An' none o' yer cheek, Miss Nellie.

MRS TRUBY-TAIT. Of course I promise, Flossie. I promise never again to try to invent things.

F

FLOSSIE. That's right, ma'am. I'm satisfied. Now I'll side up yon mess. [*She goes out.*

MRS TRUBY-TAIT. Well, Miss Jamieson, I——

MISS JAMIESON. And now I'm afraid I must tear myself away. [*She shakes hands with Mrs Truby-Tait.*] I'm really most grateful for a most interesting and fruitful afternoon. Good-bye, Miss Flittergold——

MISS FEATHERGILL [*as she shakes hands*]. Feathergill.

MISS JAMIESON. So sorry. Good-bye. Good-bye. [*To Angela*] And good luck in the Festival.

NELLIE. I'll come to the door with you. I think you're a real sport. But when you do hear Angela sing——

[*She goes out talking with Miss Jamieson. None of the three who are left is prepared to start conversation. Finally Miss Feathergill takes the initiative.*

MISS FEATHERGILL. You know, I think I quite liked Miss Jamieson.

MRS TRUBY-TAIT. She might have made things very embarrassing for us. My mind won't be quite at rest until I've seen the article in print.

ANGELA. But, Mum, you really mean it, don't you? Mean what you said about our careers and such things? You really are going to be interested at last?

MRS TRUBY-TAIT. But of course I mean it, darling. You heard me promise Flossie; you heard me dictate a statement for the *Medborough Herald*. I realize now, darling, that I've been very selfish. Of *course*, if your voice is really good you must have it trained. You must work hard, have lessons, practise——

ANGELA. And you won't grumble or complain about the noise?

MRS TRUBY-TAIT. Of course not, darling. We can arrange for you to have a room to practise in. And that reminds me, Feathers. That idea of Miss Jamieson's about sound-proof doors was very interesting. Now I wonder . . . [*Re-enter*

Nellie.] I think if I gave my mind to it . . . And it would be helpful to dear Angela . . . I think I could work out something useful—my pad, Feathers. [*Miss Feathergill goes to the writing-table and secures pad and pencil. Mrs Truby-Tait babbles on.*] We should need a double layer of felt . . . a dark green . . . well, I don't suppose the colour will matter . . . we can cover it with Beaver-board . . . [*Taking pad, etc.*] Thank you, Feathers. Now if the felt were tacked down on the outside of the door, making allowance for the hinges . . . and then there's the problem of the knob. . . . If we invented some way—— [*She is beginning to draw and scribble.*

NELLIE [*warningly*]. Mother!

MRS TRUBY-TAIT. Yes, darling? Is it very important? Because Mummy is rather busy, and if only her darling could wait. . . . Let me see . . . if the felt is thirty-six inches wide . . .

NELLIE. ⎫
ANGELA. ⎬ Mother!

MRS TRUBY-TAIT. Please, please, children. Come and talk to me some other time. Mother's busy now.

[*She returns to her scribbling.*
[*Nellie exchanges a look with Angela and moves determinedly to the door.*

MISS FEATHERGILL. Nellie, where are you going?

NELLIE. To fetch Flossie!

QUICK CURTAIN

EVERYBODY COMES TO MABEL

A VERY LIGHT COMEDY

by T. B. Morris

CHARACTERS

ESTHER, *a maid*
FAITH CAMBERLEY, *Mabel's companion*
DAPHNE, *Mabel's daughter*
MABEL KNOWLES
SONIA LANCASTER
PEARL WILLISON
DESDEMONA CIANVELLI, *a prima donna*

SCENE: The drawing-room of the Knowles' house in St Benedict's Crescent, London. Evening.

EVERYBODY COMES TO MABEL

A well-furnished room with a table telephone which is buzzing as the curtain rises. For a moment the room is empty; then Esther, a maid, enters and takes up the receiver.

ESTHER. Yes, this is ... No, she isn't. I mean she's at dinner ... Er—well, I'd rather not disturb her—she's very particular about her dinner. [*Looking through the open door*] Oh, here's Miss Camberley coming—her companion—will she do instead? ... Then I'll take a message, shall I? What name, please? Mrs Lancaster. I'll tell Mrs Knowles you'll come round, madam.

[*Esther replaces the receiver and makes a note on a pad as Faith, a quiet, youngish woman in unobtrusive evening dress, enters. Faith sits, and at once begins work on some knitting she is carrying, with little apparent interest in anything else. That is, she does not look up often, no matter what happens, though she is often ready with the right word as she works placidly through to the end of the play.*]

A Mrs Lancaster wants to see Mrs Knowles——

FAITH [*without interest*]. Oh——

ESTHER. I wouldn't bother her now because she's at dinner——

FAITH. Oh——

ESTHER. But she's coming round in a few minutes——

FAITH [*dryly, not looking up*]. I suppose you mean that Mrs *Knowles* is at dinner, and Mrs *Lancaster* is coming round?

ESTHER. That was what I said.

FAITH. Was it?

ESTHER. It was what I meant, anyway. One of these days you'll be a bit too clever. [*With dark meaning*] I know you——

FAITH [*placidly*]. Well, I don't need introducing to myself. You may go, Esther.

[*Esther hesitates as though she would like to say more. Faith ignores her existence, however, so she contents herself with making a face at Faith's back, and goes off. After a moment the telephone buzzes again, but Faith, knitting, takes no notice of it. Daphne, a healthy young woman full of brawn and briskness, in her middle twenties and Girl Guide Officer's uniform, enters and takes up the receiver. She is eating an apple, and talks through bites.*]

DAPHNE. Yes—Miss Knowles speaking. Who? . . . What? I'm eating an apple, that's why . . . I say, I'm eating an apple, that's why! . . . What? . . . Oh, you want Mother. She's just finishing dinner—yes, so am I. Life's just one rush—duty, and all that—no time for meals. I'm a guider—no, not a glider, a—no, no, not Mother—me . . . Well, can I take a message? Who are you? Do I know you? Well, I meet so many people—oh, you'll come round . . . Who? Mrs who? How d'you spell it? W—I—double L—I—T—no, S—S for simplicity—O—N. Mrs Willison——. Oh, I remember, you're the one who had that very quaint hat last week——. Oh, I don't remember *where*. And when exactly will you be round? Soon—what's that mean? Might mean anything. Must be accurate—people are too slack—and Mother thinks she's a very busy woman. Fifteen minutes? O.K.! 'Bye. [*Puts down the receiver and writes on the pad.*] Vague—un-business-like—if she meant fifteen minutes, why not say so at first? And if you'd answer the 'phone occasionally, Faith, when the servants are out, you'd save me a lot of trouble. I'm rushed to death as it is. Here, there, everywhere, doing everything for everybody . . . What, someone else coming as well? Why does Mother allow herself to be bothered with all these people? Everybody comes to her, and she imagines she is capable of advising them ... Fifteen minutes, Mrs— Mrs—— [*She hesitates, tapping her forehead with the apple.*

FAITH [*quietly*]. Willison.

DAPHNE. All right. You needn't prompt me. I know.

[*Mabel enters fussily. She is a kindly, middle-aged woman in evening dress, always trying to straighten other people's affairs and always in a muddle with her own.*

MABEL. Oh, there you are, dear! I'm so glad you haven't gone to your Band of Hope——

DAPHNE. How often am I to tell you, Mother, that it's——

MABEL. Well, never mind what it is, dear. The important fact is that, whatever it is, you've not gone to it. And so you'll be able to help me find them——

DAPHNE [*her mouth full of apple, rapidly*]. I can't stop—I'm due there now and punctuality is especially essential in officers——

MABEL. What is what in what?

DAPHNE. —especially essential in officers—and I've been already hindered with your 'phone messages and every one else's laziness. Besides, we're holding the meeting to-night in our garage——

MABEL [*blankly*]. Your garage? I didn't know you had such a thing——

DAPHNE. —and they can't get in until I go down with the key ... Oh, I mean *our* garage, not the Girl Guides' garage. Can't anyone understand anything?

MABEL. But what about the car?

DAPHNE. Don't worry about that. We can easily push it outside——

MABEL. Oh, you can, can you? I never gave you permission to use the garage—[*vaguely*] or did I?

DAPHNE. No—Father did.

MABEL. Your *father*! My dear child! [*Dismisses him with a gesture.*] Now stop talking nonsense, and tell me what it was I was going to ask you to do for me.

DAPHNE. Whatever it was, I've no time. Here!

[*Daphne thrusts the pad at Mabel, and turns to go off. Mabel grabs her arm.*

MABEL. I know—my glasses! How can I read this without them? What is it, anyway?

DAPHNE. Floods of women coming to see you——

MABEL. What?

DAPHNE. Two, anyway.

MABEL. When?

DAPHNE. Soon, I suppose. But I must——

MABEL. Why?

DAPHNE [*impatiently*]. Because I'm overdue at my meeting——

MABEL. Oh, not why you, why the women?

DAPHNE. Lord knows! To weep all over you, I expect. Let me go, Mother, do! We're doing knots to-night, and——

MABEL. You're not doing knots until I've found my glasses. I can't sympathize properly without them—and you know how people rely on my sympathy.

DAPHNE. Oh——

MABEL. Besides, if you're a Boy Scout or whatever you are you should be willing to do good turns—that's all they're for, isn't it? I mean—and remember, anyway, that charity begins—— [*Releasing Daphne*] Tying people in knots, indeed, and your poor mother as blind as a newt——

FAITH. Bat.

MABEL. Bat—what? Are *you* sitting on them? [*Ejects Faith, searching the cushions of her chair, without result.*] You always are sitting on things I want—knitting needles and scissors and—— [*Moves away to search elsewhere, Faith placidly resuming her seat.*] There's a perpetual conspiracy in this place to hide my glasses——

DAPHNE. Well, they're not here. And I must go. I've

positively got to teach four-and-twenty Brownies the sheep-shank——

MABEL. Four-and-twenty—the what? Doesn't sound proper——

[*Esther enters, the glasses in her hand. Daphne escapes and runs off.*

ESTHER [*holding out the glasses*]. Are you looking for your spectacles, mum?

MABEL [*looking at her deliberately, not seeing the spectacles, resuming her search*]. Of course I'm looking for my spectacles. What d'you think I'm looking for—the Albert Memorial?

ESTHER. I'm sure I don't know, mum. You loses so many things. That's why I was asking.

MABEL. Oh, don't waste time asking, blockhead! Go and find them for me——

ESTHER. But here they are, mum——

MABEL. What? Well, of all the little—why didn't you say so before? Where were they?

[*Mabel grabs the glasses and carelessly puts them down on a table.*

ESTHER. On the dining-room table. Just where you took them off so's you could see to eat your dinner properly.

[*Door bell.*

MABEL. Now, who's that?

ESTHER. I expect that'll be Mrs Lancaster.

MABEL. Mrs who?

ESTHER. On the pad. Didn't Miss Daphne tell you?

MABEL. Tell me? Does anyone ever tell me anything? And would Daphne have the sense to tell anyone anything even if every one else did, which, as I say, no one does?

ESTHER [*puzzled*]. I'm sure I don't know, mum.

MABEL. No. I didn't expect you would. What does she want?

ESTHER. Who?

MABEL. Oh! the Archangel Gabriel send me patience!
This woman! This Mrs what's-her-name!

ESTHER. To see you particular, she said.

[*Door bell, more of it.*

FAITH. The responsible archangel doesn't seem to be sending
her any patience, either.

MABEL [*to Esther*]. Don't stay oscillating about here, girl.
Go and let her in! Go and—go on——!

[*Esther goes off. Mabel fusses about.*

Every one always fusses so around me. Why don't they
cultivate calm? Calm. You'd think, with my example—look
at all the people who come to me for advice—I can always
think for them because I keep my head. Remember that, Faith.

FAITH [*placidly*]. What?

MABEL [*fussing more*]. Where are those glasses? I'll swear I
had them a moment ago. Oh, dear! [*To Faith*] To keep
calm, I said. [*To herself again*] Now I've got to find them all
over again. I—oh——!

[*Esther shows in Sonia, a young and beautiful brunette in
expensive evening clothes.*

ESTHER. Mrs Lancaster——

SONIA. Good evening, Mrs Knowles. So kind of you to let
me come——

MABEL [*vaguely*]. But I didn't—did I? I mean——

SONIA. I telephoned.

MABEL [*looking at the pad*]. Oh yes, of course——

SONIA. You remember me—I'm Sonia——

MABEL. Sonia? Oh yes, of course! Delighted to see you,
my dear—you know you haven't changed a bit. They said
you were Mrs Somebody——

SONIA. So I am.

MABEL. —but I never can remember people's husbands'
surnames. [*Shaking hands*] Delighted—and how are you? Do
sit down. Now where are my glasses? I'm positively as blind
as a coot——

FAITH. Bat.

MABEL. Bat—don't keep interrupting me, Faith—without them.

FAITH. Coots are bald, not blind. And your glasses are on the table, where you just put them.

MABEL. Then why couldn't you have said so before? Really, the way I'm left to fend for—[searching] I mean, no one does anything to—ah! here they are, at last——!

[Mabel holds the glasses in her hand, and peers at Sonia. Of course. I recognize you in a moment, now. You're Charles' wife——

SONIA. Yes. But I'd rather you recognized me for myself alone.

MABEL. Oh, I do! I remember coming to your wedding. Such a pretty wedding, I thought. The bridesmaids were so lovely. [Sonia starts. Mabel realizes what she has said.] Oh, I don't mean—well, you know—present company excepted, of course. You follow me?

SONIA. I'm trying.

MABEL. And how is dear Charles?

SONIA [directly]. May I speak to you alone?

MABEL. But we are alone. [Sonia indicates Faith, who takes no notice.] Oh, never mind Faith. She's always about the place—which is more than either Hope or Charity are. We've got quite used to her now.

SONIA. Well—— [Hesitates, rises, walks about, lighting a cigarette.] It's rather difficult——

MABEL. What's rather difficult?

SONIA. About Charles——

MABEL. Oh, but all men are difficult, child. Some are worse than others, that's all the difference—I mean, look at Ponsonby——

SONIA. Ponsonby?

MABEL. My husband. John Ponsonby Knowles—but I always call him Ponsonby because I think it sounds so much more—don't you? And after all, these things do—especially with men, I mean. But, as I was saying, look at him. He's absolutely—you know—without me. I do positively everything for him—except drink his port. That's what he's doing now, I expect, instead of being here to help me advise you about—I was going to, wasn't I? That is to say, that's what you came for—er—what exactly were we saying?

SONIA. You were so kind at the wedding, and every one says you're so sympathetic, and Brenda said that Gladys told her that every one always comes to you, and Charles said— well, he thought it might be a good idea if—— *[Hesitates.*

FAITH. Take three deep breaths, and begin again.

MABEL. Take no notice of her. Her tongue runs on wheels.

SONIA. It's only that I want to—er—to tell you——

MABEL *[thrilled]*. My dear—don't tell me you're going to have a baby——

SONIA *[startled]*. Have a what?

MABEL. Well, it's not unusual with young married couples, you know. I remember how thrilled I was about Daphne, and I told positively every one. She was the most adorable little thing, and—— *[Daphne enters abruptly.*

DAPHNE. Oh, for heaven's sake, is there any string, cord, twine, rope in this inefficiently run and utterly disorganized house?

MABEL *[placidly]*. Why, dear? Do you want to hang yourself?

DAPHNE. But it's no good asking you. You'd think the little fools would bring their own—— *[Daphne runs off.*

MABEL. Oh, dear, every one bothers me—but, my dear, I don't mean, of course, that you—now what were we saying? Oh yes, Daphne—what was I saying about Daphne?

FAITH *[dryly]*. She was the most adorable little thing——

MABEL. I wish you wouldn't keep butting in, Faith. Now you've got Sonia all muddled up, and she was just telling me —if you'd rather whisper it, dear——

SONIA. I don't want to whisper anything. It's only that I've decided to leave Charles. [*Pause.*]

MABEL. Leave? . . . But I thought you were going to say —but never mind . . . My dear child, you can't possibly have got tired of him yet——

SONIA. It isn't that. I've met someone else.

MABEL. Do you mean someone better? Charles is a dear boy——

SONIA. But this is the only possible person. I—I mean— well, have you ever been really in love?

MABEL. In love? I married Ponsonby, and I've put up with him for thirty years. If that isn't love, I don't know what is.

SONIA. Love is something great and glorious, transfiguring the whole of life, painting all the drab colours bright, making everything seem fresh and wonderful——

FAITH. Like spring-cleaning.

MABEL ⎫
SONIA ⎭ What——?

FAITH. Spring-cleaning.

SONIA [*making a face, persisting*]. Something absolutely over- whelming. I didn't go out of my way to seek it. I—I—well, I was just——

FAITH. Unavoidably overwhelmed.

SONIA. —just carried away. Of course I told Charles at once. I'm sorry for him, poor boy. You see, it isn't really his fault——

MABEL. No, I can see that.

SONIA. —so I came to tell you, because he said it might be a good idea—and of course I want to do everything I can for him.

MABEL. Of course. [*Pause, then Mabel continues brightly*] I see—you want me to try to persuade you to stay with him?

SONIA [*aghast*]. Oh no! You can't do that! I'm telling you I've met the one love of my life and——

MABEL. Well, I can't persuade you to run away from him,

can I? I mean, it isn't done—that is to say, persuading isn't done. One can't go about persuading young wives to leave their husbands every time they meet the one love of their lives, and——

SONIA. Oh dear! Aren't you going to be a little helpful?

MABEL. You must be very sweet and self-sacrificing, my dear. Renunciation is such a beautiful thing——

SONIA. In theory——

MABEL. There's a wonderful passage about renunciation in —what's-its-name?—you know, that thing by—by—by—who-is-it? I know exactly what it is. There's a copy of the book in the library—at least, that's where it ought to have been when I saw it last. I'll get it for you, and I'm quite sure it'll help you to renounce Charles—no, no, I don't mean that! I mean, to renounce the greatest love of your life, and *resume* Charles——

SONIA. But I don't want——

MABEL [*very patiently and seriously, taking Sonia's hands*]. It isn't what we *want*, child, that matters most in life. I found out that about Ponsonby—I mean—well, think of Romeo and Juliet, and Héloïse and—er—what's-his-name——?

FAITH. Abélard.

MABEL [*gesturing impatiently to Faith*]. —and Florence Nightingale, and—er—Daniel and the lions, and——

FAITH. Goldilocks and the three bears.

MABEL [*to Faith*]. What nonsense are you talking now?

FAITH. Well, I don't suppose she wanted bears any more than Daniel wanted lions.

MABEL. But what on earth's that to do with—what were we talking about——? Oh, renunciation——

FAITH. As much as Daniel had—it was *the lions* who did the renouncing——

MABEL [*with a gesture of giving Faith up as hopeless*]. Well, talking of that—or thereabouts—I know one test of patience that *Job* wouldn't have stood—— [*To Sonia*] I'll go and get it—the book, I mean. Don't take any notice of Faith. She always was a little mad, and I'm sure she's much worse lately, since she's been living with us—I won't be a minute——

[*Mabel rushes off. Faith knits placidly.*

SONIA. Is she always like this?

FAITH. Yes.

SONIA. Don't you mind?

FAITH. No.

[*Sonia, exasperated by Faith's placidity, moves about restlessly. Then she makes another attempt.*

SONIA. What are you doing?

FAITH. Knitting.

SONIA. Yes—but what?

FAITH. A sweater.

SONIA. For yourself?

FAITH. No.

SONIA [*looking*]. Oh, for a man! [*With a note of excitement*] I say—you aren't in love with him, are you?

FAITH [*without the least enthusiasm*]. Yes.

SONIA. Is he very handsome?

FAITH. No.

SONIA. Well, I expect he's clever, then?

FAITH. No.

SONIA. You are talkative, aren't you?

FAITH. No.   [*Door bell.*

SONIA. Someone's coming. Perhaps I'd better go. [*Pause.*] Do you think I'd better go?

FAITH. Yes.

SONIA [*uncertain*]. Oh! Why?

FAITH. You've made me drop two stitches.

[*Esther shows in Pearl, a young and beautiful blonde, in expensive evening clothes that contrast effectively with Sonia's.*

ESTHER. Mrs Willison—oh, Mrs Knowles isn't here, then?

FAITH. Library.

PEARL. Am I intruding?

FAITH. It doesn't matter. I've gone wrong already.

SONIA. She means with her knitting.

ESTHER [*to Pearl*]. Will you please sit down? I'll tell Mrs Knowles.

PEARL. Thank you.

> [*Esther goes off. Sonia is looking hard at Pearl.*

SONIA. What did you say your name is?

PEARL. I didn't—the maid did. Pearl Willison.

SONIA. Oh——

PEARL. But perhaps I'd better go. I—I didn't know I was intruding——   .

SONIA. Oh, don't go! You're not—I'm sure you're not! I'm just off, anyway. I only looked in to ask Mabel's advice——

PEARL. Did you? That's funny—so did I. She's so helpful —at least every one says she is. Every one says how good and understanding——

SONIA [*sighing*]. I'm afraid she isn't very understanding to-night.

FAITH. Advice is never helpful unless it's taken.

> [*Pause, Sonia and Pearl looking at each other. Then both speak together.*

SONIA ⎱
PEARL ⎰ What have you——

> [*Pause. Each realizes that she is being rude.*

SONIA ⎱
PEARL ⎰ Sorry! I—er—I mean——

SONIA ⎱
PEARL ⎰ I think I'll go——

FAITH. I can knit to conversation, but not to choral verse.

> [*Sonia and Pearl open their mouths to begin again, but clap their hands over them, each trying to give the other a chance. They laugh.*

SONIA [*breaking away*]. I say—have you ever been in love?

PEARL. Yes—I—I—oh!

> [*She sits on the nearest chair, bursting into tears.*

SONIA. What's the matter? Don't you like being in love?

PEARL. No.

SONIA. Why ever not?

PEARL. It's my husband——

SONIA. Oh, don't mind him. Nothing should stand in the way of real love—the most glorious experience that life has to give.

FAITH. Except the next one——

SONIA. What?

FAITH. Experience.

SONIA [to Pearl]. Don't you worry about him——

PEARL [desperately]. But you don't understand! It's him —my husband—that I love, and I'm so m-m-miserable I could——

SONIA. What?

PEARL. I don't know.

SONIA. Miserable? But why? If you're in love with him, look at all the trouble you're saved. It's so much more difficult to be in love with someone else's husband.

PEARL. But he's going to leave me. There's another woman——   [Sonia starts.

SONIA. What? Is he going to run away with her?

PEARL. No. She's going to run away with him. She's a——

SONIA [hastily]. Do you know her?

PEARL. No. I wish I did.

SONIA. Why?

PEARL [fiercely]. So I could scratch her eyes out, the vixen! Just imagine! She's married already, but, not content with one perfectly good husband, she must have two—the greedy, grasping, covetous—trollop!

SONIA. Here, I say! . . . I—I mean—she can't be all that——

PEARL. She's more. She's a useless, worthless, dolled-up siren; a shameless, soulless snatcher of—oh, how I'd like to get at her!—but I shall, some day. David can't hide her away from me for ever. One day I shall get her, and then——

G

SONIA [*alarmed*]. What?

PEARL [*significantly*]. Let her just wait——

FAITH. Damn! I've dropped another stitch——

PEARL. *She* won't have a stitch left to drop.

SONIA. But—I say! Has it occurred to you that you may be judging her harshly——?

PEARL. Give me a chance to condemn her harshly——

SONIA. You don't even know what she's like, you say——

PEARL. I know she must be old and experienced—to seduce my David away from me—poor boy. Painted on top—old underneath. Lamb dressed as mutton—no, no, I mean——

[*Mabel enters, brightly.*

MABEL [*rapidly, to Sonia*]. So sorry, my dear—but the strangest thing happened. I went into the library, and there was poor dear Ponsonby—asleep, with—what do you think? —the *Continental Bradshaw* on his—[*points to her stomach*] waistcoat. Poor darling, he must have mistaken it for a book —a natural error, for I don't think he's ever—I mean, I'm not even sure that he *can*—there are the papers, of course—but then, they have *pictures*, so that isn't—is it? . . . Where was I? Oh, I was so intrigued that I completely forgot what I went for. I just stood there and chuckled and chuckled, and he was quite peevish when I—but tell me, dear, what *did* I go for? [*Seeing Pearl*] Oh, hullo! Now let me see——

PEARL. You remember me. I'm Pearl Willison——

MABEL. Do I? Yes, of course I do—it all comes back wonderfully. Such a pretty wedding. The little page in blue velvet with the lace—adorable—until, of course—but they always will, won't they? I mean, either they eat too much, or else——

PEARL. I had two—they were both sick. But that was afterwards. Anyway, it doesn't matter now——

MABEL. And you've lived happily ever afterwards——

PEARL. I don't mean that——

MABEL [*suddenly excited*]. Ah! Was it you who had the interesting piece of news?

PEARL [*blankly*]. News?

MABEL [*whispering loudly*]. Little stranger——

PEARL. Little what?

MABEL. Isn't it you? But I'm sure someone said that—you know, the stork, and——

PEARL. Stork?

MABEL. —and I do so adore other people's babies——

PEARL. Babies?

MABEL. Then I don't think it can be you—oh dear, then someone must have gone wrong somewhere. Well, never mind, I dare say I shall—and meanwhile, what can I do for you two? Do you know each other?

PEARL. No.

MABEL. This is Sonia——

PEARL [*starting*]. *Sonia?* Sonia who?

MABEL. Let me see—Charles' wife. Now, why do I think of the Wars of the Roses? I can't just——

PEARL. *Sonia Lancaster?*

SONIA. I think I'll leave you to your little chat. [*To Mabel*] Thank you so much, dear, for helping me.

PEARL. Are you the female who's trying to steal my husband?

MABEL. S'sh, my dear! You mustn't talk like that. I mean, don't call a lady a—and I'm sure she doesn't mean anything of the kind, really. [*Waving them to silence*] I mean—well—when anyone talks about everything being fresh and new, like spring-cleaning, one always knows it's only a passing fancy, doesn't one? [*Suddenly waking up to the full situation*] Oh, do you mean that it's *your* husband that *she's* running away with——?

PEARL [*grimly*]. She *thought* she was running away with him. But there won't be enough of her left to run anywhere with anyone——

[*Pearl advances on Sonia, ready for battle. Mabel gets between them.*

MABEL [*agitated*]. Now, now, please! Don't—don't do anything—I mean, rash! You may do something you'll regret if you do anything you'll be sorry for. I mean—let's talk it over, shall we? In spite of dear Mr Chamberlain's—er—I always think appeasement is—you know——

[*Daphne enters abruptly, taking no notice of anyone else.*

DAPHNE. Mother—where is the bicarbonate of soda? One of those little idiots has eaten——

MABEL. Didn't the gardener have it for that wasps' nest?

DAPHNE. —and now she's—no, that was cyanide of potassium—oh dear, doesn't anyone ever know anything?

MABEL. Come here, Daphne, and stop Pearl from killing Sonia. After all, you *are* a good turn, aren't you?

DAPHNE. I can't. I'm going to murder a whole company of Brownies—— [*Daphne rushes off.*

PEARL } [*together*] { Let me get to——
SONIA }   { Keep her away from——

MABEL [*struggling to keep them apart*]. My dears, you must be sensible! How can I hope to advise you if you keep *pushing* so?

PEARL. How dare this abandoned baggage try to tempt my husband away from me?

SONIA. How dare you call me names? Abandoned baggage, indeed! What do you think I am—the lost property office?

PEARL. You seem very fond of finding other people's property before it's lost——

SONIA. Not lost, isn't it? You wait and see! It's your own fault, anyway. You shouldn't leave your husband lying about without attention——

PEARL. You predatory little cat!

SONIA. Is that insulting?

PEARL. I hope so.

SONIA. You don't want him yourself, and you won't give him a chance to better himself——

PEARL [*outraged*]. *Better* himself!

SONIA. You're a dog in the manger—no, not a dog, a——

PEARL. And you're another—only not a pure-bred one——

MABEL. Girls, girls! [*Makes a great effort and pushes them on to the settee, one at either end, and stands over them.*] Now be good! Sit still now, and we'll have a nice conference—find a way out of this. There is a way out of everything, you know, if you—and don't forget what the poet said: The tongue is mightier than the sword.

FAITH. Which poet?

MABEL. Be quiet, Faith! If you don't know, it's about time you did. Now—Pearl's husband has fallen in love with Sonia——

PEARL. He hasn't! It's only a low intrigue she's trapped him into——

SONIA. How dare you call me an——

MABEL [*stopping her*]. Come, come! . . . And Sonia is in love with Pearl's husband. That leaves Pearl and Sonia's husband on the shelf, so to speak . . . [*Thoughtfully*] Now I wonder—of course the easiest solution would be——

PEARL [*angrily*]. Are you going to suggest that I take her cast-off husband?

MABEL. My dear, how clever of you to guess. [*Ruefully*] But there, I suppose that wouldn't really work——

PEARL. Well!

SONIA. Oh, I'm sure Charles couldn't stand her. Besides, he's never looked at any woman except me.

PEARL. How do you know that? I thought David was the most faithful man on earth—and now I find he's carrying on a barefaced intrigue behind my back with a common little——

SONIA. Are you calling me a common little——

PEARL. I'm going to—you're a—ah, you would, would you?

[*Sonia has thrown herself on Pearl, and they are beginning a beautiful fight, with Mabel clucking about like a distracted hen, and Faith knitting placidly, when Desdemona enters with Daphne and Esther. She is an imposing Italian lady of middle age, expensively dressed. Her movements and gestures have all the magnificence of grand opera. Her lightest word is directed for the back of the gallery, and her effect in a drawing-room is that of a battleship in a duckpond. Daphne and Esther have evidently been trying to dispute her entrance, and she is literally sweeping them before her with outspread arms. She sweeps them to the centre of the room.*

DESDEMONA. Ah, morte! You stoppa me? You blocka my way? Insects! Imbeciles!

[With a final push, Desdemona deposits Daphne and Esther on the settee, on top of Sonia and Pearl, regarding the resulting mass of waving limbs with the contempt of a big-game hunter for his kill. One almost expects her to place a triumphant foot upon them and be photographed. Magnificently she brushes them off her hands. Meanwhile:

MABEL ⎫   ⎧ What?
SONIA ⎬ *[together]* ⎨ Here, I say——
PEARL ⎭   ⎩ Oh!——

DAPHNE. Mother, who is this woman? She insisted——

ESTHER. She would come in, and she wouldn't be said no to, mum.

[They sort themselves out, watching Desdemona, who expands, preparing for verbal action.

DESDEMONA. I come!——

MABEL. Evidently. But—er—if one may ask—why?

DESDEMONA [*rapidly*]. Thisa man—thisa turncoat, traitor, breacher of promises—thisa *trifler with me*! Where 'e is?

[She gesticulates fiercely to all in turn, except Faith, and they recoil.

MABEL. Who?

DESDEMONA. I tella you. I am come for 'im. I teach 'im to breach 'is promises. I—ah bella donna!—I makea 'im wish 'is papa and mama they 'ad never met.

MABEL. But who? Why?

ESTHER [*at the telephone*]. Shall I ring for the police, mum?
[*No one takes any notice of Esther.*

DESDEMONA. You aska me why? Is it not wrote all over me
[*expanding*] that I am an injured woman? I trusta 'im—'e
letta me down—*boomp!* Ah, the scorpion!

MABEL. Let you down?
[*All except Faith get near again, interested, to be swept back
in turn.*

DESDEMONA [*passionately*]. You calla me a liar? You
believea me not? Do I look like a liar—me, Desdemona
Cianvelli, prima donna? A liar? 'Ave I not sung before all
the crowned 'eads—and the others—of the 'ole world? 'Ave
I not sweepa audiences off their feet an' carry them away?
[*She sweeps them.*] La Cianvelli as Traviata—exquisita! La
Cianvelli as Aida—superba! La Cianvelli as Carmen—
perfecta! La Cianvelli as Marta—magnifica! La Cianvelli as
Francesca da Rimini—ah bellissima! [*Sobbing*] La Cianvelli
as Mimi—pathetica! [*Simpering*] La Cianvelli as Madama
Butterfly—oh, *so* sweet! I 'ave— [*Indignantly again*] But 'ave
I come to tella you this?

FAITH [*coolly measuring her knitting*]. You're asking *us*?

DESDEMONA. No! I come to finda that worm; that miserable, insignificant, sneaking little sneaker of a forsworn
imitation of a lover—ha! An' when I find 'im—*oh, what I doa
to 'im!*

ESTHER [*snatching off the receiver*]. Police . . . Whitehall 1212.
[*Daphne snatches away the receiver and jams it back.*

DAPHNE. It's not the *police* we want——

MABEL [*to Desdemona*]. Er—this is all very interesting—I'm
sure—but if you would please explain——

DAPHNE. I must get back to my Brownies. They're all tied
up in sheepshanks and sheetbends—besides the one who's——
[*Daphne runs to the door but stays there, curious. Pearl and
Sonia are laughing silently behind Desdemona's back, but
hastily stifling laughter when she turns in their direction.*

Esther remains near the table, clutching it, half bewildered,
half frightened, occasionally slipping round it out of the way.

DESDEMONA. Sheep's eyes! That is what 'e makea at me,
this betrayer!

MABEL. But who?

DESDEMONA. 'E was to meet me at Victoria. We were to
go south together [*ecstatically*] to the sun of the Riviera—the
mimosa—the blue, blue sea——

MABEL [*interested and sympathetic*]. Blue, blue, blue—yes——

DESDEMONA. —and the little clicking counters of the
croupier at the Casino—ah, bellissima, the sun! I likea not
this England with 'er fogs and 'er policeamen. [*Angrily again*]
We were to go together, I say—together—and now this—
this—this—oh, this miserable sinner e' leava me to go alone!

MABEL. Alone! How sad!

DESDEMONA. 'Alf of one hour I 'ave waita at Victoria and
'e 'ave not arrive. Ah, morte, morte! I will cut 'im into one
little piece for every minute I 'ave wait.

MABEL [*trying to grapple with the situation*]. Do we understand that you were—er—eloping with a man?

SONIA. Eloping?

DESDEMONA. 'E call 'imself a man—this *object*!

DAPHNE. But I don't see how this concerns us——

MABEL. Won't you tell us why you came? I mean, we're
delighted to welcome such an—er—well, I mean, distinguished
—and—but——

DESDEMONA. I comea because 'e live 'ere.

DAPHNE. But there's some mistake. There isn't a man in
the house—except Father.

[*Pearl and Sonia are startled out of their mirth. Pearl grips*
Sonia's arm.

MABEL [*mildly*]. No. So there isn't! I never thought of that——

DESDEMONA. Then you must be 'is wife. 'E 'ave a wife—
she understanda 'im not. [*Angrily*] 'Ave you keep 'im from
the fond arms of 'is true love?

MABEL. Is every one going mad?

FAITH. Of course. I told you that for a long time.

MABEL. What?

FAITH. That every one in this house is mad.

MABEL. Oh, be quiet, woman!

FAITH. Don't call me woman!

MABEL. Here am I, being told that my husband, who never did a thing for himself in the whole of our married life, is running away with this—this——

[*At a loss for words, she makes a sweeping gesture at Desdemona, who recoils.*

DESDEMONA. But that is just what 'e is nota doing, the deceiver. 'E breach 'is promise.

DAPHNE. But you can't run away with Father! Think of the scandal! Think of my position in the Girl Guides——

DESDEMONA. When I, Desdemona Cianvelli, makea up my mind, I am stoppa by nothing. I takea no notice of your Girla Guides.

MABEL [*helplessly*]. Oh, something must be wrong some-where——

PEARL [*giggling*]. If you ask me, I think everything must be wrong everywhere.

MABEL. Ponsonby can't be deceiving me. He wouldn't dare. Besides [*with a glance at Desdemona*] he always hated loud women.

DESDEMONA [*shouting*]. You calla me what? I am not a loud woman!

MABEL. It must be someone else. What is this man like?

DESDEMONA. 'E is a pig.

DAPHNE. Father is *rather* like a pig.

MABEL. Be quiet, child! This is no time to make obvious remarks about your father.

SONIA [*to Mabel*]. Didn't you say that your husband had been reading a *Continental Bradshaw*?

[*All except Faith and Desdemona stiffen in amazement.*

MABEL [*alarmed*]. Oh!

DESDEMONA [*joyfully*]. Then all is well, and 'e 'as nota breach me. Where is 'e? Let me goa to 'im——

[*She starts off. Mabel drags her back.*

MABEL. What is this man like?

DESDEMONA. Oh, if 'e 'as nota deceive me, 'e is a man—my great, fond, mighty lover! So strong! So 'andsome! So—ah, bellissima! I *melt* in 'is arms. [*She melts into the arms of Esther, who is behind her and is nearly overwhelmed. Daphne is starting to the rescue when she recovers.*] Takea me to 'im——

MABEL. Half a minute, my good woman! You may be a great opera star, but——

DESDEMONA [*furiously*]. I ama not a good woman——

MABEL. —but you can't come into other people's houses and walk off with their husbands without a by-your-leave——

DESDEMONA. I walka not. I never walk. I takea da cab.

MABEL. And poor dear Ponsonby hasn't even the imagination to *think* of being unfaithful to me. Besides, he always tells me everything——

DESDEMONA. 'Is name is not Ponsonby. It is Ben. I calla 'im Benito for short——

MABEL. Oh, this is too much! Don't I know my own husband's name?

DESDEMONA. Pah! You English wives you know nothing at all about your 'usbands. 'Is name is Ben, and 'e livea at [*ticking off on her fingers*] 101 Saint Benedict's Place. Ben—Benito—Benedict—so I remember.

[*Mabel has run to the table and taken up a photograph.*

MABEL. Look! Is he like this?

DESDEMONA. This is nota your 'usband——

MABEL. Nota what? Great heavens, woman, *don't I know my own husband?*

[*Pause; Sonia and Pearl are nearly dead with suppressed laughter.*

PEARL [*weakly*]. But this is St Benedict's *Crescent*——

SONIA [*weakly*]. Not St Benedict's Place——

FAITH. —and cast off fourteen . . . [*placidly underlining the obvious*] You've come to the wrong house.

DESDEMONA [*blankly*]. Is it possible that I, La Cianvelli, 'ave made a mistake?

[*Pause. Desdemona obviously deflates. Mabel, who in her own crisis has lost her earlier mental woolliness, now secures the wind that has left Desdemona's sails and becomes truculent. She advances slowly on Desdemona, who retreats before her step by step all round the room.*

MABEL [*rapidly*]. Mistake? I'll say you have, you conceited, overblown cabbage of an operatic has-been, you! You comea here—I mean, you *come* here, trying to make me believe worse things of my dear husband than I believed already—I mean, well, you know what I mean—you female cockerel, crowing about your crowned heads and your successes. Madama Butterfly, indeed!. I'd like to stick a pin through you. I'd like—I—O heaven, send me breath and inspiration!

DESDEMONA. Signora, do not makea da scene, I beseech! If you will but listen, I will makea da apology and takea myself off——

MABEL. You takea yourself off first——

DESDEMONA. But I cannot go likea this? This is no exit line for me. I am prima donna——

MABEL [*rushing at her*]. Get out—or I makea you prima mincemeat——

[*Desdemona flies off, upsetting Daphne and Esther in her hurried exit. Mabel, Daphne, and Esther exeunt in a scramble after her. Sonia and Pearl, laughing, run to the door and look off. There are sundry expressive noises off, heavy bangs, and a loud slam. Sonia and Pearl cling to each other in helpless laughter, assisting each other back to the settee. Faith has been knitting stolidly throughout, and continues to do so.*

SONIA. Oh dear—I've never laughed so much—oh!—

PEARL. Her face! And Mabel spitting Italian English——

SONIA. Like an outraged organ-grinder——

PEARL. Did you ever see anything like it?

SONIA [*pointing at Faith*]. And look at her—just knitting placidly through it all and—oh, I shall die!

PEARL. I'm dead already!

> [*They collapse again into each other's arms. Then Pearl breaks away, feeling herself anxiously.*]

And I've ruined my foundation. I'm sure something went then——

> [*Stopping her laughter abruptly, changing to icy coldness.*]

Do you remember who you are?

SONIA [*laughing*]. No. [*Abruptly serious*] Oh!

PEARL [*angrily*]. How dare you laugh with me——

SONIA. You laughed with me——

PEARL. I was going to kill you, when she came in——

SONIA. So you were. [*Laughing again*] I can't help it if you are. I—oh, this is too rich!

PEARL [*shaking her*]. Stop it! I can't murder a helpless woman——

> [*For a moment she shakes Sonia, who goes on laughing; then, overcome again, she bursts into fresh laughter and collapses beside Sonia.*

SONIA [*laughing*]. Pearl—be friends! I won't have your husband. You can keep him. We've got to be friends—with such a memory. Oh, my ribs!

PEARL. You mean you'll—make him come back to me?

SONIA. Yes. I—I've heard enough about husbands leaving wives to—to last me a lifetime——

PEARL. Darling! And it was all your fault, wasn't it? I mean, he never really loved you——

SONIA [*sharply*]. What? [*Hastily discreet*] That's right, dear. All my fault. We will be friends, won't we?

PEARL. Yes. We've so much in common——

> [*They kiss. Mabel enters, followed by Daphne and Esther.*

DAPHNE [*grumbling*]. And if all those poor children have hanged themselves in knots—as they may well have done, the little fools!—you'll be to blame. One of them's certainly burst without that bicarbonate——

MABEL [*her old self, placidly*]. Oh, don't be so funny, Daphne. Here we are having terrible adventures, and you can only think of trivialities . . . Well, that's that—except that I'd like to be there when she gets to the right address. And now, girls, we'll resume our interrupted—er—you know what I— and let me see now—what exactly was it we were talking about? [*Enlightened*] Oh yes. I remember perfectly. Now which of you was running away with the husband of which?

SONIA. It doesn't matter——

PEARL. We're friends now——

MABEL. Then you aren't—he isn't—she isn't—they're not——

SONIA } [*clasping each other*] { No. No husbands are ever
PEARL } { coming between us again.

MABEL. Oh, I'm so glad, my dears. [*Anxiously*] But—er— not exactly so—er—close—you know what I mean? There are limits—that is to say, well, after all, poor dear boys, neither of them married *both* of you——

SONIA. Oh, it was too good! That woman—and you— and Faith sitting and knitting——

MABEL. Oh, faith might move mountains, but nothing will move Faith. But of course she was right for once. I saw through the woman immediately. You know—a mistake. I mean—poor dear Ponsonby. Why, do you know that, in all our thirty years together, he's never once answered me back. Let that be an example to you—not Faith, of course, she hasn't one—I mean, never give your husbands a chance to answer you back and—well, now everybody's happy, and——

FAITH. —and the next row begins ten more cast off. [*Rising and folding up her work deliberately*] Don't be too sure. I think the time has come for me to tell you something——

MABEL. Oh, don't talk so much, Faith——

FAITH. You're so fond of trying to advise other people that you've never advised yourself to treat your husband like a man and not like something to be kept in a box and called "poor dear Ponsonby." Ponsonby, indeed! How'd you like to be called Ponsonby for thirty years?

[*All tense, staring. Faith stalks to the door and turns there.*] Do you know why he was reading *Bradshaw*? That fool Italian woman made another mistake. She was two hours too early for her train—*and ours.*

[*Faith goes off. The others faint in various directions.*

CURTAIN

HER AFFAIRS IN ORDER [1]

by Mada Gage Bolton

"Judith Morley, of Foxsprings, Texas, convicted and sentenced to life imprisonment for the killing of her employer, Colonel Basil Patterson, also of Foxsprings, was pardoned to-day, after serving ten years of her sentence, as she is dying of a fatal disease.

"The pardon, reviving the sensational story of the young housekeeper who killed the World War hero, by stabbing him to death, is granted that the doomed woman may return to her home, and put her affairs in order."—*News item.*

First produced by the International One-Act Play Theatre at the Vaudeville Theatre, London, on November 8, 1936, with the following cast:

Beth Morley	HEATHER MCINTYRE
Abbie Morley	ALICE DARCH
Linda Morley, a teacher	GRIZELDA HERVEY
Miss Brant, a reporter	AUDREY HENDERSON
Bailey, a prison nurse	BEATRICE ROWE
Judith Morley	JEAN SHEPEARD

The Play produced by GODFREY BAXTER

[1] From the collection *Three Prize One-Act Plays*, published by Messrs George Allen and Unwin, Ltd.

CHARACTERS [*as they appear*]

BETH MORLEY, 22, *youngest of the four Morley girls; pretty, sweet, and appealing*

ABBIE MORLEY, 33, *eldest save Judith; married, mercenary, intensely afraid of what "people will say"*

LINDA MORLEY, 29, *once lovely; moody, untamed, restless, entirely selfish, difficult; a school teacher*

MISS BRANT, 27, *reporter from Dallas; canny, and efficient at her job*

BAILEY, 55, *prison nurse; portly, gentle, and compassionate*

JUDITH MORLEY, 35, *once lovely, now thin, face drawn—from frequent unbearable pain—but still retaining definite traces of looks; beautiful voice*

TIME: An April afternoon

PLACE: Foxsprings, Texas (a fictional town), about sixty miles from Dallas

HER AFFAIRS IN ORDER

SETTING: *Judith Morley's bedroom, in the old Patterson home, once an elegant, grand old show-place, now retaining unmistakable glimpses of this past.*

Starting from D.L., there is a marble-topped chest of drawers, with a mirror above it. A door C.L. wall. The bed is extreme up L., foot towards proscenium. Beside the centre-side of this bed a small table with a quaint old lamp upon it. Then, somewhat R. of centre-rear, is the door to the hallway.

The R. wall, about a third of the way down, juts suddenly into a triple-windowed bay, the three windows having venetian blinds, which are lowered.

D.R., facing these windows, is a large comfortable chair, stool before it, and small table up-stage of it.

The blinds, which are not entirely closed, shed thin bars of sunshine on to this chair group.

The bed is naked of covering, the rest of the furniture being in dust-covers, presenting a strangely ghostlike appearance.

The stage, which is deserted, remains so a few seconds; then a key is heard in the lock of the rear door. The door opens, and Beth, arms full of clean linen, enters, turns, and gently closes the door with her knee, and crosses to lay her load on the bed. She is sobbing, and seems half afraid of the room. Presently she goes about, taking dust-covers off things, ending at the chest D.L., which she dusts with the covers in her hand, and of which she presently opens the top drawer and, sobbing still more, begins to take toilet things from it, wiping them carefully, and placing them on the marble top.

The rear door opens explosively, and Abbie stands there.

ABBIE. Beth! Oh, there you are. [*Beth, startled, turns.*] Now, whatever are you blubbering about? [*Beth turns back to her task without replying, and Abbie comes into the room towards the chair D.R., stopping suddenly behind it with a little cry.*] Good Lord above us!

BETH [*turning*]. What's the matter?

ABBIE [*points to the chair, with bars of sunlight playing over it as the blinds swing gently*]. Look at the bars! Bars—waiting for her!

BETH [*crosses, and raises the blinds, flooding the chair with sunshine*]. Bars! Just sunshine. I think she'll be glad of a little sunshine.

ABBIE [*slightly recovered*]. Well! The bed not even made— what *have* you been doing all day?

BETH [*with quiet resentment*].. You told me to let everything wait—till the children were got off. [*Sounds of a car outside are heard; Beth turns to look out of the window.*] It's her! It's Judith, Abbie! A big car—no! [*Abbie is crossing.*] No—it's that newspaper woman from Dallas—the one who was here before—there's a man with her—he has a camera! [*Beth whirls on Abbie accusingly.*] That's why you're letting her come to-day—to take pictures of Judith! You, who talk of living things down, do this!

ABBIE [*looking down from the window sombrely*]. I didn't ask Judith to come home! [*She crosses to the bed, and speaks after a few seconds.*] Why did she have to come back? To rake everything up for us again—just as people had begun to forget. For ten years we've lived things down—tried to make them see we hadn't been to blame.

BETH. Then why are you letting that woman come?

ABBIE [*shaking out a sheet on the bed*]. Because she's paying me well for it. If Judith is coming back, money will be needed —more than Dick can spare.

BETH. Judith wouldn't want you to get money that way! Money's your God—you'd do anything for it.

ABBIE [*turning, furiously*]. Go to your room and stay there! Stay there till I send for you! God knows I've enough on my mind to-day without your romancing!

BETH. I won't! Can't you realize Judith's coming home— to die? No—I see—you don't! Well, I do, and I'm going to make those people leave—[*starts to run for door, rear*] if I have to——

ABBIE [*whirling, catches Beth's arm, and flings her back into the room*]. You'll do nothing of the sort! [*Beth bursts into sobs.*] I'm surely not to blame if Judith killed a man!

BETH. I don't believe she did it! I never have!

ABBIE [*wearily*]. And what would you know about it— and you only twelve years old when it happened?

BETH. I knew Judith——

ABBIE [*with quiet bitterness*]. She killed him. I remember hearing voices in her room—at first they sounded as if they came from Linda's room, and I thought at first Judith had been scolding Linda again for letting Colonel Patterson give her so many things, or running away to Dallas with him the day before. Then I heard *his* voice—angry—and I could never bear his anger, so I kept to my room—I heard a crash —I couldn't move. Soon my door opened, and Judith leaned there, and looked at me with wild eyes, and held out the— knife she did it with—a Mexican one someone had given her. I fainted when I saw blood dripping off it.

BETH [*has been sobbing during story*]. Then she had some good reason—he was a beast! I was quite glad, I remember, when I knew he was really dead!

ABBIE [*sardonically*]. And that your sister—had killed him!
[*Begins finishing the bed.*

BETH. Oh, no!
[*The door, L., opens, and* LINDA *stands there, looking from one to the other darkly.*

LINDA. You must have heard a car drive up—there's some-one downstairs, and you up here rowing like a couple of dogs! [*To Abbie*] She says she's a Miss Brant from the *Dallas World-Telegram*, and that you're expecting her. There's a photographer with her.

ABBIE [*taking things in hand*]. Beth, go to your room, wash your face, and tell that woman I'll be right down. I've got to finish making this bed. Remember, Beth [*Beth has started out*]—no foolishness, or it will be harder on Judith.

LINDA [*after Beth is gone, crosses to window*]. What have you been badgering Beth about now?

ABBIE [*crossly*]. None of your business! I thought you were leaving?

LINDA. I changed my mind. If moving into the next block would save me from gossip—but it wouldn't. I guess I'll stay, and if the School Board wants to fire me for being a Morley, let them. [*Bitterly*] Sometimes I wish fervently they would!

ABBIE. I suppose you do! Well, if you think Dick can be saddled with another Morley bringing in no money!

LINDA [*with quiet hate*]. Don't think I'd stay here—that's why I wish sometimes they *would* fire me—then I'd have to get out of this dry-rot town.

ABBIE. And what would you do then?

LINDA. I don't care awfully! [*Before Abbie can expostulate*] When will she be coming?

ABBIE. The Warden's letter said about three.

LINDA [*looking at her watch*]. It's going on to a quarter past now.

ABBIE. Good Lord!

LINDA. Will she be coming in an ambulance?

ABBIE [*putting the finishing touches to the bed*]. I don't know, I'm sure. Linda, take these dirty things downstairs, and tell Miss Brant if she wants to see this room before——

LINDA. What is the paper paying for a pre-view of Judith's room?

ABBIE. Now, Linda, I don't want to—— [*A knock on the rear door, and Linda reaches and opens it. Miss Brant stands there.*]

Oh! [*Abbie's voice gets gentler instantly, taking on the air of a martyr.*] Miss Brant!

MISS BRANT. Yes—I found time was slipping ,away, and she'll be here soon, so I just followed your voices up. [*Looks about.*] This is—her room?

ABBIE. Yes, I've been sort of touching things up a little.

MISS BRANT [*walks in, looking about, stops D.L., and turns, her eyes lighting on Linda*]. Yes.

ABBIE. I don't believe you have met Linda, Miss Brant— she is the middle sister.

MISS BRANT [*eyeing Linda with interest*]. You are the sister who has not visited or written Judith Morley these ten years. Why?

LINDA [*flashes Abbie a furious glance*]. What did they pay you for that, Abbie? [*Sombrely to Miss Brant*] I do not consider it any concern of yours.

ABBIE [*hastily, to cover Miss Brant's discomfiture*]. Linda was Colonel Patterson's favourite—from a tiny child, when we first came here—our father was the Colonel's overseer—the Colonel always petted her—that is why she could not understand her sister killing him.

LINDA. You know nothing at all about it, Abbie! [*To Miss Brant*] I was not only his favourite—I was the only one who didn't hate him. I happened to be grateful. When Father died we had nothing; he kept Mother on as housekeeper—when she went, he kept Judith so we would not be separated or starve.

MISS BRANT [*deciding to capitalize on the quarrelsome tension*]. Miss Morley, have you during these years any new ideas concerning the motive for your sister's deed?

LINDA [*witheringly*]. No—I have not! My sister here is the one who'll sell you theories for money!

MISS BRANT [*watching Abbie's control*]. I see—sorry—I know it is a tender subject. [*Turns to Abbie.*] So this is the room where he was found?

ABBIE [*moving away suddenly from the bed, and looking back to where she stood*]. Yes, there, just inside that door, at the foot of her bed.

MISS BRANT. That door—where does it go?

LINDA [*before Abbie can answer*]. To my room. [*Suddenly, half mockingly as a barker in a carnival*] You've not seen all of Judith's room! Her bed, her dressing-table, her chair—even her telephone, just as she left it! [*To Abbie, scornfully*] Abbie! Judith's extension left in all these years? Twenty-five cents a month for ten years—that's thirty dollars! How extravagant of you! [*Rushing on, half hysterically*] You have a photographer with you! While we are waiting for Judith's arrival, would you like pictures of the three of us? We've not been photographed together since we were children with our ponies!

MISS BRANT [*has had about enough of Linda*]. Mrs Taylor, there are a few things you were vague about the other day that I must get settled before she comes. If you can help me now——

ABBIE [*apprehensively*]. Yes, what are they?

MISS BRANT [*looking at notebook from purse*]. I have all the information about her condition from the prison infirmary. It's cancer, and, since the excitement of being pardoned, her heart has complicated the situation definitely——

ABBIE. You mean—she may go any time?

MISS BRANT. Wouldn't that be a mercy, with cancer?

LINDA. My sister was thinking of the saving in money, I'm afraid, Miss Brant.

MISS BRANT [*angry at last*]. Mrs Taylor, we made certain arrangements with you the day before yesterday—if they were not satisfactory, I wish you would tell me so at once.

ABBIE. Please forgive us—we are all upset—we only heard about the pardon three days ago ourselves.

MISS BRANT [*contrite*]. I'm sorry, of course; it was sudden.

Now, I have the photographer in the dining-room, as we planned—the curtains are drawn. When she enters the front door he'll get a quick flash; she'll know nothing of it till it's over.

ABBIE. Yes—that is best.

MISS BRANT. Now—she mailed a letter to you from the prison yesterday. What was in it?

ABBIE [*reluctantly*]. It said—not very much, Miss Brant—just that she hoped she wasn't going to be too much trouble —that we wouldn't mind.

MISS BRANT [*after the slightest pause, biting her lip in disappointment*]. That was all there was—in it?

ABBIE [*promptly*]. That was all.

LINDA. Didn't she say how happy she was to be here for Beth's wedding?

ABBIE [*impatiently*]. She did not!

MISS BRANT. And that, you say, is put off.

ABBIE. Naturally, with her sister so ill—Beth would not want to marry and go away.

[*Linda laughs hollowly to herself.*

MISS BRANT. You don't mind—that she is coming home, do you? You *are* glad she needn't die in prison?

ABBIE [*with great effort*]. Naturally.

LINDA. Yes, our family has always been very proud. [*Mockingly*] A murder now and then—but to die in prison for it—much too much!

[*Telephone is heard ringing off-stage.*

ABBIE. Linda, please go down and answer that.

LINDA [*turning with a half smile, picks up Judith's extension*]. Yes—Hello—we have it upstairs, Beth. Long distance? Yes —Dallas calling? Yes, this is the Taylor house—yes—Judith Morley's home—oh, you mean Miss Brant—yes, she's here —one moment. Your editor, I believe, Miss Brant.

[*Miss Brant crosses and takes the receiver as Beth rushes in and flies to the window.*

BETH. Abbie! Linda! She's coming! A big grey car just turned the corner from Laurel Street!

[*Miss Brant puts her hand over the transmitter for a moment, and leans towards the window, as Abbie and Linda cross upstage for her to look.*

MISS BRANT [*into transmitter hurriedly*]. Hello, George—hold everything a moment! Just a sec.!

LINDA [*bitterly*]. Well, she certainly has an audience, hasn't she?

ABBIE [*in horror-stricken tones*]. Look! People pouring out of the houses! The whole town has been waiting—I felt them all morning, straining behind curtains! Damn them! Oh, damn them!

LINDA [*calmly*]. They're no worse than we. We're doing the same.

BETH. A nurse is getting out!

ABBIE [*as shouts can be heard*]. What are they saying?

LINDA. They're shouting welcomes! Our Judith's a heroine —ten years, and every one forgets she killed a man—in cold blood!

BETH [*turning suddenly, slaps Linda*]. You're a beast! She had a good reason—I know she had!

MISS BRANT [*to Beth quickly*]. Do you know the reason?

BETH. No. And if I did, I wouldn't tell you. [*Starts for the door.*] I'm going out to meet her.   [*Exit.*

ABBIE [*recovers and starts out, too*]. Yes, let's get her in quickly.   [*Exit.*

LINDA [*crosses to her door, L., turns with a half sneer to Miss Brant*]. You will have a grandstand view from the windows there, but, as a favour to the family, be out of here before they bring her up.

MISS BRANT [*hand still over transmitter*]. Why, you damned, cheeky—— [*But Linda is out, her door closed.*] [*Hand off transmitter, talking rapidly, as she watches from window*] Hello, George —is Eddie on the line, too? Good—now get this down—she's arriving. No ambulance, touring car from the prison—looks like the Warden's. Nurse and assistant with her. Now, climb down! I know what time it is, and I couldn't call you any sooner. Listen—[*with weary impatience*] are you going to waste my time and yours—not to mention toll charges— telling me what you think of me? Let me talk! They're helping her out of the car now. Has on a grey light coat, dark dress underneath—can't see her face—too many people! Sure, she has a hat on! Black! Sports hat! Whole town present—poured out of adjacent houses when car drove up —waiting all morning. They're shouting welcomes to her! Sure, people forget—besides, she's dying, isn't she? They're clearing a way to the porch—God, what a racket! Listen, George, only angle we can use is human interest. Nothing new—every one about her accepted theory she was his mistress —and fact he left everything to the girls and herself cinched that belief. No, she wouldn't talk at the prison—don't expect her to here. Now I can see her! [*Pause*] Yes, I'm here—God, she's still beautiful—pale and very thin, but you'd know her from those old pictures! Eyes like holes burned deep in a blanket! Sure, the photographer is waiting, ready to shoot as she steps in the door—and a car is waiting outside to run the pics up to Dallas! Got to scram now—I'm in her own room, and I hear them coming in the door downstairs! Can't talk any more—got to scram, I said! Cheerio! Sure, I'll call you from the hotel before I leave.

> [*Bangs up receiver, puts phone down, rushes to rear door, looks out, slips out, closes door.*
>
> [*Stage is vacant for a moment, then Abbie enters with Bailey, the prison nurse, in white regulation nurse's garb.*

BAILEY [*pausing to look round*]. So this is the room?

ABBIE. Yes, this is—her room. Shall we bring her up to it?

BAILEY. Not yet, for a moment. I had to see you alone; that's why I asked to come up first. I—wanted to prepare you.

ABBIE [*apprehensively*]. Prepare me?

BAILEY. Yes. Your sister may not live the night. [*Abbie, who has been standing near the foot of the bed, sinks limply on it.*] She's too far gone—this heart defection, of course, was the final straw. She overworked during a recent epidemic in the prison infirmary—collapsed one day, and we found her condition. How she'd gone about even we can't understand.

ABBIE. I didn't know cancer could kill one so young— she's only thirty-five.

BAILEY. I'm sure I don't know. [*As Abbie paces to and fro*] At any rate—I may be mistaken—probably am. And she won't be here long enough to cause any trouble. We had a near accident on the road, and she nearly went then. Only her determination to get home alive has enabled us to bring her to you.

ABBIE [*controlling herself again*]. Maybe, then, we'd better leave her downstairs. .

BAILEY. Don't even suggest it. For years she's told me about this house—this room, how she'd always lived here, and had expected—wanted to die here. It's all that has kept her alive till now.

ABBIE. I see—well—it's ready.

BAILEY. Here are her medicines. [*Takes a small case to the little table D.R.*] I must get this prescription made up immediately—we used most of it on the road. It's for her heart. When she has an attack—some drops in water—about ten —repeat in half an hour if necessary. I tell you this in case I am not around when something goes wrong.

ABBIE. In case you are not around?

BAILEY. These tablets are for pain—when it gets unbearable. Yes—didn't they write you I was going to stay for the first few days?

ABBIE. No—I hadn't planned.

BAILEY. I have grown very fond of your sister—I'd like to see her through. She thinks they're making me stay— but I'm really taking my holiday early.

ABBIE. I don't know if we can find room.

BAILEY. Then I'll get a room in the neighbourhood.

ABBIE [*fearful*]. No, you mustn't do that—you'll stay here! Beth'll share her room with you.

[*Beth enters, then goes back to door, looks off R., her face beaming.*

BETH [*to Bailey and Abbie*]. It's Judith—she's coming up the stairs all by herself! She wouldn't let anyone help her! Isn't that splendid! Good, Judith darling! You're almost up!

BAILEY [*peremptorily brushing Abbie aside, starts for door*]. Good God! She'll never make it!

[*But Judith appears at the door, catches on to the frame to steady herself, and smiles at Bailey.*

JUDITH. I did, though, Bailey! I did! [*She is breathing with difficulty, and her eyes, ignoring the persons in the room, go about hungrily.*] How big! Oh, Bailey, I'd forgot it was so big! [*Starts into room; Bailey rushes to her; she refuses aid.*] No, Bailey!—please don't help me. Isn't it just like I told you?

BAILEY. Yes, Miss Judith, just as you told me it is. I'd have known it anywhere.

JUDITH [*has reached the back of the chair D.R.; stands there, looking out of the window*]. My windows! Sunshine and trees to watch, streets with children playing, and people going past! Bailey, isn't it lovely!

BAILEY [*coming to her determinedly*]. It'll be lovelier if you'll sit down and take it easy at first.

JUDITH [*as a tear drops on to her hand*]. Bailey! You're crying!

BAILEY [*simulating crossness*]. That I am not! Calm yourself down, now; that climb was enough to have finished you straight.

JUDITH [*suddenly afraid*]. Bailey, don't let me die yet! I've just come home.

BAILEY. Of course we won't. You can't do that to us after all the trouble of bringing you. [*Dropping bluff*] How do you feel?

JUDITH. A little tired—not too tired.

BAILEY [to Beth]. A glass of water, please, at once.

[Beth exit, rear.

JUDITH. I'm glad they're making you stay with me a little while, you know. Of course, the little Mexican woman may be having her baby any day now—it's selfish of me.

BAILEY. Never believe that woman! That baby won't come for two weeks.

JUDITH [quietly]. Is that all the time—I've got left?

BAILEY [takes the glass of water Beth hands her; drops medicine into it]. You're Beth, aren't you? Well [as Beth nods] take this prescription down to the nearest drug store. Wait for it. [Frames words "Hurry, please," and Beth leaves quickly.] Now, here you are—down with it—just in case you overdid coming up those steps. That was a damfool thing to do.

JUDITH [takes the medicine, and leans back, smiling]. Was it, Bailey? Oh, no.

BAILEY. I'm the judge of that! No more back talk.

[She smooths Judith's hair gently.

JUDITH. What did the Governor mean in my pardon by saying I was freed that I "might return home and put my affairs in order"?

BAILEY. Oh, I don't know—nothing probably; some legal term.

JUDITH. I see.

BAILEY. Now you rest here in the sunshine while I go down and get our things from the car, and see them started back. They've a long journey.   [Exit.

JUDITH [as she hears Abbie leaving]. Abbie?

ABBIE [stopping]. Yes, Judith. [She turns finally and goes D.C.] What can I do?

JUDITH [after a moment, not looking round]. You don't mind my coming home, Abbie?

ABBIE. I wasn't asked—I was just told, Judith. Of course

it isn't easy, everything being raked up again—and this time Dick and the children share in the notoriety.

JUDITH [*wincing, tries to change subject*]. Oh, the children, Abbie—why haven't I seen them?

ABBIE. We thought it best to send them away—they're with Dick's mother in Lancaster—there was so much talk, and they're just as full of questions as——

JUDITH. Abbie, I see. I shouldn't have come home—and I didn't think of it that way—I've been selfish—but it wasn't my idea—this pardon; they gave it to me. I didn't ask; they offered it to me, and I so wanted to see Beth married—and the children——

ABBIE. It isn't myself I'm worrying about. And this is as much your home as ours—it was left to all of us.

JUDITH. I'm glad you could keep it—I was afraid after my conviction they might try to get things away from the rest.

ABBIE. If he'd had any relatives to contest the will—they probably could have. It caused a good deal of talk—but I've been glad since, too, that we could stay here. Dick makes very little——

JUDITH. I haven't seen Linda—where is she?

ABBIE. She's probably in her room there. Shall I call her?

JUDITH. Not just now—tell me about her. Is she happy, teaching?

ABBIE. I don't think Linda likes anything. She hates teaching, the town, the people. She is very difficult. She stays only because she can't save enough money to get away. Spends everything she makes on herself.

JUDITH. Why hasn't she married?

ABBIE [*with scorn*]. Who'd marry such a shrew? Bitter and sarcastic she is—I don't know how she keeps her job.

JUDITH. Abbie, I had to come, when they offered me the chance. If I can only live till next Wednesday when little Beth is——

[*A knock on door, rear, and Beth enters.*

ABBIE. Here's Beth now.

BETH [*handing Judith the bottle, which she unwraps*]. There you are, darling. Henderson fixed it himself while I waited—he sent his regards. [*Judith, holding the bottle, stares at Beth, warming under her smile.*] Abbie, Miss Brant is back—she has something for you, and asks if you could see her a moment.

ABBIE. Yes, I'll go down now. I'll be back—later, Judith.

JUDITH [*as Beth sits on the stool at her feet*]. Little Beth, so soon to be married and leave us. Tell me about your Jim. He was in knee breeches when I last saw him, with a noseful of freckles.

BETH [*laughing*]. Oh, the freckles have all gone now, Judith! He's sweet, and wants to come up to see you as soon as you will let him.

JUDITH. Yes, I must see him.

BETH. Shouldn't you rest? We have plenty of time later to talk. [*Rises.*

JUDITH. No, dear—please. Don't leave me alone—I've been so long alone. So long.

BETH [*sits again, taking Judith's hand*]. I know, dear; it must have been terrible.

JUDITH [*leaning back, her eyes closed*]. No—not too terrible. You just stop living, actually—except in the past realities. People remain as they were to you, before you left them, and things seem to sort of pause somehow—waiting.

BETH. Yes, dear.

JUDITH. In prison everybody has something in common—something that held us together, sympathetic with each other, long after the cause of our being there was forgotten. The habit of just existing became so regular and continual. I didn't realize that I would come back to find things so different. I childishly thought what I did—had—hurt me— most of all. I find—I was very wrong.

BETH [*jumping up*]. What has Abbie been saying to you? Don't pay any attention to her.

JUDITH [*very happy for a moment*]. All right, Beth. Tell me more about your Jim. Where will you live?

BETH. On Laurel Street—just round the corner—the old Jenkins place. His mother had it remodelled for us.

JUDITH. It must be lovely. I remember the catalpas when they bloomed in the spring.

BETH. Yes, it is lovely. We were going to Galveston for two weeks after the wedding.

JUDITH [*quickly*]. Were? Have your plans changed, Beth? [*With a swift laugh*] Don't tell me you're going to Niagara as newly-weds used to do? [*Starts another laugh, to stop abruptly in the middle of it, as Beth refuses to meet her eyes.*] You haven't——

BETH. The wedding is put off—Judith—indefinitely. So —let's not talk about it any more.

[*Rises and walks to the window.*

JUDITH [*suddenly seeing the trouble*]. Why was the wedding put off, Beth? [*Beth is silent.*] Why was the wedding put off?

BETH [*after a moment*]. It was his mother. It wouldn't have made any difference to Jim—he's decent and sweet, but his mother holds the purse-strings—he has to do what she says. She says we must wait——

JUDITH. Until—I am gone? [*Beth, in the midst of sobs, nods. A knock comes on door, L.*] Yes, yes—come in!

[*Judith is staring at Beth in hurt bewilderment, and does not turn to see who has entered. It is Linda.*

LINDA. It's Linda. [*Beth leaves in tears.*] I see Beth has told you Mrs Coombes won't let them marry till your coming has died down a bit.

JUDITH [*presently*]. Linda, come round where I can see you.

[*Linda crosses to C.*

LINDA. I suppose you find us all very changed.

JUDITH. I'm afraid it's I who have changed, and I didn't know it.

LINDA. No, it's us; you changed us—by what you did.

We could never be the same after that. [*Suddenly*] Why did you have to kill him? He was going to give me everything —and you took it from me! I'll never forgive you!

    [*Linda crosses in front of Judith and stares down out of the window.*

JUDITH. Was he—going to give you everything?

LINDA. Of course. You angered him that night you burst in upon us—that is why he said he wasn't going to marry me. I'd have got him to—I'd have been all right—your over-developed maternal sense—I always said it would get you in trouble!

JUDITH. Did you really think you—a child twenty-five years younger than he—could make him marry you?

LINDA. Yes—and you spoiled my life for me.

JUDITH. *Spoiled* your life for you?

LINDA. Yes, he would have given me this house—everything would have been all mine; instead I have to slave at teaching half-witted farm children!

JUDITH. He had mentioned marriage to me—but I never believed him. I knew he was rotten through——

LINDA. You were jealous because he turned to me.

JUDITH. I had warned you. But—I hadn't told you why I was so sure the way you were going led to grief.

LINDA. You led me to grief, not I!

JUDITH [*stiffens, then speaks tersely*]. Remember the emergency appendix operation I was rushed to Dallas for, two years after mother died? Well, it wasn't that at all; it was something else—he had threatened to put us all out—you three were so small, I was frightened, I—believed him. [*Linda is staring.*] Yes, Linda, I was going to have a baby— but I didn't—and now because the operation wasn't done properly I'm dying for it. He's killed me after all—he's avenged himself on me! [*Linda is slowly backing round Judith, who rises with great effort as she continues*] I warned you— you wouldn't listen. That night I heard him in your room.

He used to come to mine—until I kept Beth in to sleep with me. I heard him, and I came in. He laughed——

LINDA. He laughed at you for interfering.

JUDITH. Oh, no! He laughed when I asked him if he intended marrying you—if he had told you he would. I went blind, raging mad. [*Judith is up, holding on to the back of her chair; Linda has backed almost C.*] I didn't know I had strength to plunge a knife into a man, and then to drag him in here. I got him out of your room. I knew I was finished, but I thought you could be saved—I thought the shock of it would bring you to your senses, so I kept quiet, and let them say anything they wanted. [*Morosely*] You kept quiet, too. *You* could have saved me.

LINDA. What could I have said?

JUDITH [*a brittle laugh*]. What could you have said! I had killed a man to save you——

LINDA [*fiercely*]. I hadn't asked you to—I still hate you for it!

JUDITH [*wilting slightly, holds more securely to her chair, her head down, breathing with difficulty*]. Yes, you still hate me for it! That's the bitterest thing of all. You weren't worth it —you weren't worth saving! I've lost ten years of my life —I didn't know, but they were to be the last ten years—to save someone not worth it! Oh, God in heaven, it hurts to think——

[*Suddenly she gasps, turns frantically, trying to get back to her chair, collapsing in front of it. Linda screams, steps are heard outside, and, as Linda stands staring at Judith, Bailey rushes in.*

BAILEY [*not seeing Judith at first*]. I heard something fall— Oh, good heavens, Miss Judith! [*Bailey rushes to Judith, drops to her knees, takes Judith in her arms.*] The medicine in the blue bottle! Quick! No, there's none there—get Beth and find the fresh supply! [*Beth rushes in.*] The new medicine you got! And a glass of water! [*Linda exit for water as Abbie comes in.*] Miss Judith, darling, what did you try to do now?

I

JUDITH [*opening her eyes*]. Bailey, take me back to prison, quickly! Let's go back!

BAILEY. Take you back! Nonsense, you're in your own home, where you belong.

JUDITH. No, I must go back—I did wrong to come home —I—— [*She is struggling for breath.*

ABBIE. No, you can't go back now—it would cause more talk.

BAILEY. Can't you find that bottle, Beth?

BETH. No, I gave it to her. [*Coming round, drops to her knees beside Judith to the R.*] Judith, dear, I gave you the new bottle. What did you do with it?

JUDITH. Beth, promise me that you will marry next Wednesday as you have planned—please—promise—quick— Beth!

BETH. Judith, I couldn't——

JUDITH. Little Beth, don't keep me—I *want* to go. Promise——

BETH. I—promise, Judith. I promise.

JUDITH. Abbie—I'm sorry—I didn't—just realize. One can't ever—go back—I didn't know—how—impossible— forgive—— [*Suddenly she stops, gasping for breath; her face takes on a gentle smile; she raises one hand towards Bailey—in it is the missing bottle.*] Bailey, dear—if this is what—you're looking—for——

[*As Bailey reaches hurriedly for the bottle it slips from Judith's hand, crashing to the floor as she slides from Bailey's arms. Bailey reaches desperately to feel the pulse that is no longer there, and, with Abbie and Linda standing looking down, and Beth sobbing into Judith's hair,*

CURTAIN

INTERMEZZO

by Vincent Godefroy

CHARACTERS

THE PRIMA DONNA
THE MAID
THE LADY

SCENE: The Prima Donna's dressing-room at the Opera House.

NOTE: The music that plays an important part in the background of this play consists of the finale to Act II, Scene 1 and the opening of Act II, Scene 2 of *La Traviata*. At the rise of the curtain the closing of the aria *Di provenza* is heard, and when the music is resumed at the end of the play it continues till the final curtain falls. It must start loud enough to be striking, and may then be softened out of all prominence.

The necessary music will be found on these records:

H.M.V. C 2221—end of first side and beginning of second, *or* *Columbia* 9636—end of second side, and *Columbia* 9637— beginning of first side.

The slight but important musical allusions in the play will at once be explained by a hearing of these records.

Another record that may be useful is *H.M.V. E* 573, including the sounds of an orchestra tuning up, the noise of an audience, and applause.

INTERMEZZO

THE SCENE *is the dressing-room of the operatic star, Bianca Mari-nuzzi. The door is at the back, towards the R. Diagonally across the room, but somewhat towards the back, is a divan, littered with bright cushions and discarded costumes. In front, against the L. wall, is a dressing-table and folding mirrors. Opposite, inclined away from the R. wall, is a writing-desk. The room is not tidy. Dresses hanging or lying about suggest a comfortable jumble. There is a woman seated at the dressing-table, wearing a period ball-room costume, painting her lips. Behind her stands another, putting the finishing touches to an elaborate arrangement of hair—presumably the Prima Donna and her Maid. Behind the scenes can be heard music—the closing aria of* La Traviata, *Act II, Scene 1. It is faint, but distinct.*

PRIMA DONNA [*in perfect English*]. Not bad, Edwards . . . not bad.

MAID. I didn't think I could make you look so beautiful.

PRIMA DONNA. Edwards . . . what exactly do you mean by that?

MAID. I was amazed at how lovely you look to-night.

PRIMA DONNA. Are you complimenting me, or yourself?

MAID. Why, you of course; but myself just a little. I don't get many kind words in this world, so I sometimes have to supply my own.

PRIMA DONNA. I suppose that's a subtle allusion to my temper, Edwards.

MAID. Well, now, there's a compliment straightaway. Nobody's ever called me subtle before.

PRIMA DONNA. So now we're quits. [*The music stops.*] Hallo, there goes the applause. Old pot-bellied Mercadante is bowing obsequiously in all directions. Personally, I think his voice is atrocious—I don't know about you?

MAID. I don't pretend to be a judge. I hate opera.

PRIMA DONNA. Is there anything you like?

MAID. Not much. I enjoy paddling. And I don't object to a glass of stout.

PRIMA DONNA. Two very intellectual pursuits, Edwards.

MAID. Is that another compliment?

PRIMA DONNA. You can take it as you like. I've never indulged in either myself; but then I'm not intellectual.

MAID. I suppose you're fishing for me to say you are?

PRIMA DONNA. You've as good as said it.

MAID. Indeed I haven't.

PRIMA DONNA. You know, Edwards, I don't think I would recommend you to anyone as a maid.

MAID. I hope you won't.

PRIMA DONNA. You're too . . . well, you talk a bit too much.

MAID. What ought I to do? Sit and look pretty?

PRIMA DONNA. You could sit.

MAID. Wait till I've finished your hair.

PRIMA DONNA. Oh, I think you have. I look exactly what I'm supposed to be. A thoroughly loose woman. Abandoned —that's the right word, isn't it?

MAID. I'm sure I don't know. I'm not up in such words. But I'm glad you're satisfied with the result. We must be successful to-night. And this Hewitt woman is about due.

PRIMA DONNA. Hm. And do you think I look all right?

MAID. Good enough for the Hewitt woman, I am sure.

PRIMA DONNA. Do I look exactly as I should—like a woman with a past?

MAID. I've done my best. But I've never had a past.

PRIMA DONNA. No, Edwards, I'll believe that much of you. But it's my past that is the point to-night, or so it seems. It's all very exciting, this odd Hewitt woman claiming that I was once a friend of hers, earning my living on the pavements. All very exciting. I suppose she really wants some money.

MAID. I have no doubt.

PRIMA DONNA. You know, Edwards, if she looks down-trodden I shall be half inclined to give the poor devil something and send her away.

MAID. What? Is there to be no fun?

PRIMA DONNA. I am sure you'll get fun out of it whatever happens.

MAID. You aren't nervous?

PRIMA DONNA. No . . . no . . . of course not. But . . . well, it's an unfortunate night for this woman to have chosen. Here I am all dressed up for *La Traviata,* playing the part of a loose young lady—just the type she claims to remember me as. Is this expensive dress and wig enough? If only she had come last night when I was Madam Butterfly. She wouldn't have had a leg to stand on. But to-night, here I am, hardly disguised; Bianca Marinuzzi to the world, Kathie Woodward to this one miserable woman.

MAID. You're beginning to lose heart at the last moment. I thought our plans were cut and dried. This sort of person must be taught a lesson. She's to get away with nothing. I wish it was me she was after. I'd let her have it!

PRIMA DONNA. No. I'm not losing heart. Why, it's nearly seven years ago she says she last saw me. All I've got to do is to hold out and refuse to recognize her, till she goes off baffled. You'll be sitting at the desk, writing letters and stone deaf. Don't for heaven's sake forget you can't hear what's going on. I'll deal with her . . . and if I haven't succeeded in showing her the door by the time the next scene starts, well . . . we stake everything on Flora's voice down on the stage. As soon as Flora sings, you can undeaf once again.

MAID. You're banking on her not knowing the opera. What if she does?

PRIMA DONNA. My dear Edwards, it's all a gamble. She's

gambling just as much, and I'm counting on that. But *she* won't know the opera. As long as she thinks I ought to be on the stage before it's my call, we've got her. So don't *you* start having doubts at this late hour. I'll do all I can to get rid of her during the interval, but I shan't be afraid if I don't succeed. The opera will do the trick.

> [*There is a knock on the door.*

Here she is! Come on, Edwards! To the desk! And don't forget you are deaf . . .

MAID. Don't forget it yourself.

> [*She sits at the desk and starts writing.*

PRIMA DONNA. Come in!

> [*The door opens and the Lady enters. She is flashy in dress and war-paint. A very tawdry edition of the Prima Donna's made-up character. She stands still for a moment, and then advances. She speaks with a Cockney accent which every now and again she makes a brief effort to conceal.*

LADY. Miss Bianca Marinuzzy?

PRIMA DONNA [*from now affecting Italian intonation*]. Signorina Bianca Marinuzzi, at your service.

LADY. I'm charmed. I've brought you these flowers. They ain't . . . aren't much.

PRIMA DONNA. They're very beautiful. I am deeply touched.

LADY [*suddenly confident*]. 'Aughty, ain't you, Kathie Woodward?

PRIMA DONNA. I beg your pardon?

LADY. You 'eard, Kathie Woodward.

PRIMA DONNA. Am I speaking to Miss Hewitt?

LADY. You know damn' well I'm Mickey Hewitt, and don't pretend.

PRIMA DONNA. Miss Hewitt, I have received a very strange letter from you. I'm afraid I could not understand it. The grammar seemed unusual—but of course I'm not English. What exactly is your business?

LADY. Can your maid go?

PRIMA DONNA. It's all right. She's very deaf, poor dear.

[*The Maid at the desk smiles to herself. Indeed, throughout the scene her expressions can play an important part, as she wavers between amusement and anxiety.*

LADY. And needs to be, with all the caterwauling that goes on in this joint. Say, Kathie, how ever did you get hitched up with this swell gang?

PRIMA DONNA. Will you *not* address me as Kathie! State your business.

LADY. You haven't forgotten me, have you?

PRIMA DONNA. I've never seen you before, so what is there to forget?

LADY. Never seen me before? You dirty liar.

PRIMA DONNA. What was that?

LADY. I said, you dirty liar. I'm afraid I don't speak Italian. You remember me well enough, I'll lay.

PRIMA DONNA. I am very glad to say I don't.

LADY. You'll soon be sorry to say it.

PRIMA DONNA. You presume to know me?

LADY. Yes, I know you. You changed a bit, but not much. Money can alter any face.

PRIMA DONNA. And so can a good slap, Miss Hewitt.

LADY. The same proud Kathie of East Street.

PRIMA DONNA. Miss Hewitt, in your letter—so far as I could make out—you claim to have been a friend of mine in less happy days. May I say that I have never set eyes on you before, that I have never heard of you, that I have never mixed with women of your type, and that my time is extremely short?

LADY. You may say what you like, Kathie. But only one thing you said is true—and that is, your time is short. Very short, Kathie, if you don't come round.

PRIMA DONNA. You really are a very remarkable person. Have you come here to murder me, or what?

LADY. I'm not so daft. I'm just here to let on to you I know who you are. I haven't forgotten the good old days we had together in East Street. D'you see?

PRIMA DONNA. I do not see.

LADY. Oh yes, you do, but you don't like to. That's about what. Prima Donna! Huh!—Opera Queen! Huh!—Society darling! Huh!—I could tell 'em what lies behind the pearls and the paint. What would all the nobs say if they found out? Lords have a crush on opera singers, don't they?

PRIMA DONNA. They may. I claim the acquaintance of none.

LADY. I've heard there is some lord after you.

PRIMA DONNA. Only my landlord!

LADY. Funny. You always was a wit, Kathie.

PRIMA DONNA. I really cannot make out why you should suffer from these strange delusions. I haven't the remotest idea who you are. And you certainly do not know me. Perhaps my photograph in the papers has suggested some old friend of yours? I do not take very well.

LADY. I've got other ways of knowing you, Kathie dear.

PRIMA DONNA. You have made a very unfortunate mistake. I think you had better go before your error leads you into any indiscretion.

LADY. You've certainly learnt to talk proud. But I know you in spite of all that make-up. You look like what you are—one of us.

PRIMA DONNA. That is precisely as it should be, Miss Hewitt. I am made up to play the part of a woman of just your kind. That you should recognize this may be natural selection, or it may be a compliment to my artistic maid. Unfortunately she's too deaf to hear it.

LADY. Bianca Marinuzzi, you look pretty rich. How comes it you keep a deaf maid?

PRIMA DONNA. That is my business.

LADY. Poor sort of business.

PRIMA DONNA. Which I might say of yours.

LADY. Smart. You always was smart, Kathie Woodward.

PRIMA DONNA. Really, you are making a most objectionable mistake, coming here and claiming to know me. If you had any manners, you would understand that you have not been received as a friend. And you would apologize and go. I'm sorry for you, Miss Hewitt. It was very sweet of you to bring me these flowers. I'm sure I wish you no malice. If I can ever be of any help to you, well—you know—if you're in a fix, I'd like to do you a good turn. I hope you didn't spend much on the flowers. They're very beautiful.

[*She turns for her bag.*

LADY. That's right, Kathie—playing the lady very nice. D'you think I paid anything for them? For you? A boy left them home last night. Very convenient they came in.

PRIMA DONNA. You know, you are a little crude; but fascinating. I'd like to know more about you. We've met through a mistake. Perhaps it will turn out a lucky mistake. Sit down and make yourself comfortable. Here, I'll just move these things off the divan.

LADY [*sitting*]. That's better, Kathie. Now we can get down to business in a more friendly way. You come off your perch and we'll just swing along.

PRIMA DONNA. Oh, please don't regard me as being on a perch.

LADY. You always was trying to climb, Kathie.

PRIMA DONNA. This is most interesting, your taking me for someone else. When did you last see this Kathie?

LADY. Not since you disappeared suddenly from No. 18 East Street without so much as a toodle-oo.

PRIMA DONNA. A toodle-ooo? I . . . I'm afraid I don't quite understand. What is a toodle-ooo?

LADY. Yah, Kathie, 'sno use you carrying on with this Italian talk. See here, I know ruddy well who you are, and I know a ruddy sight better who you used to be. Kathie Woodward, you and I shared lodgings at No. 18 East Street and many's the good time we had. Many's the good catch we made down by the river. We shared both good luck and bad. We were real pals. And now they've found they can rake in big money by using your voice you're too high and mighty to recognize me. You're only the servant of some big show boss, while I am free, a lady of independence, my own managing director. Yet you look down on me as though you were higher in the world. Kathie, you're lower, darned lower. Your life isn't your own when your work fills other people's pockets. It's I should look down on you. But I don't—or at least I won't—if you'll be honest and admit who you are.

PRIMA DONNA. This is highly entertaining. I like you, Miss Hewitt. Go on.

LADY. Cor—we've had some fun, you and I. D'you remember the night I fooled the police by putting on a pair of trousers? I got you out of a sticky hole then.

PRIMA DONNA. I would be more obliged if you would get me out of the sticky hole of your imagination, if that's the sort of thing you've come here to talk about.

LADY. Ah, so you haven't forgotten it?

PRIMA DONNA. Go away!

LADY. I thought you just said you liked me?

PRIMA DONNA. I'd like you better outside the room.

LADY. Oh no, you wouldn't. Once I was gone you'd wish me back in here out of mischief. But there'll be no mischief if you tell the truth. Why, there was a night I sat by your bedside five hours while you had the belly-ache, and saved your life with hot bottles, and cheered you with stories and kisses . . .

PRIMA DONNA. Stop that indecent nonsense, and get out!

LADY. Ashamed of the memory?

PRIMA DONNA. Get out!

LADY. You know where I'll go, don't you?

PRIMA DONNA. I'm not concerned.

LADY. Yes, you are. I'll get hold of the manager of this joint and spill a few beans in his ear. Pretty tasty beans too.

PRIMA DONNA. Beans? What about beans? I don't follow.

LADY. Perhaps I should have said spaghetti. Ay'm afraid ay don't know the common talk of Italians . . . only you ain't no Italian, Kathie. Pretend all you like; I've got your secret. Bianca Marinuzzy . . . Prima Donna . . . Italian . . . I know you're not! I know you're not! I know you're not!

MAID. Signorina . . . Hasn't the bell gone yet?

[The Prima Donna shakes her head.

LADY [jumping up from the divan]. Cor, your voice gave me a fright. I forgot all about you. What's this about a bell?

PRIMA DONNA. The bell for the next scene. But it's about due. And I shall have to drag myself from your sweet company, Miss Hewitt.

LADY. Keeping your role up to the end, eh?

PRIMA DONNA. Miss Hewitt, I've been very indulgent in listening to all this rot. May I ask you a direct question?

LADY. Shoot.

PRIMA DONNA. Are you mad?

LADY. Kathie!

PRIMA DONNA. O Kathie, Kathie, Kathie . . . what is this obsession?

LADY. Obsession? I don't know many long words, but I know two and two makes four.

PRIMA DONNA. I congratulate you—if the word 'congratulate' isn't too long for you.

LADY. Saucy!

PRIMA DONNA. Saucy?

LADY. Yes. Don't pretend. You know what saucy means; spaghetti and-tomato-saucy—if you still insist on posing as a Wop.

PRIMA DONNA. Sacramento . . . you filthy little English tart! Insult my nation again, and I will drag you out of this theatre by your hair!

LADY. Hm. Roused? If you had been a genuine Wo . . . Italian, you would have sent me packing long ago. I've been impudent enough, for a stranger; but we're not strangers . . . Kathie Woodward.

PRIMA DONNA. Have you a seat in the theatre?

LADY. No damn' fear.

PRIMA DONNA. Would you like one?

LADY. Would I like one! See here, it's no good trying to bribe me out. I'm here with a purpose.

PRIMA DONNA. It's certainly time you stated your purpose. All you've done so far is to assert that I am someone else, apparently called Kathie Woodward. Now tell me, Miss Hewitt, how long ago was it that you shared lodgings with this woman?

LADY. It was seven years ago you ran away from your pitch, Kathie.

PRIMA DONNA. My maid here, Edwards, has been in my service for nine years. Ask her yourself.

LADY. It's no use if she can't hear.

PRIMA DONNA. You can shout.

LADY [approaching Maid]. 'Ow long 'ave you been . . .

MAID [starting]. Goodness gracious!

PRIMA DONNA. I said you could shout, not bawl. There is a subtle difference.

LADY [shouting]. How long have you been Marinuzzy's maid?

MAID. Eh?

LADY. Lord above! [Shouting] How long have you been Marinuzzy's maid?

MAID. No, thank you. Not to-day.

LADY [to Prima Donna]. How do you manage with her?

PRIMA DONNA. Try again. Speak more slowly. And my name is Marinuzzi.

LADY. 'Ow long 'ave . . . How long have you been Marinutzy's maid?

MAID. Oh, is that all? Let me see . . . nine years and . . . August, September, October . . . November . . . nine years and six months come All Saints. And I'm not looking for another position.

PRIMA DONNA. So you see, Miss Hewitt?

LADY. Two can lie as well as one.

PRIMA DONNA. Two can tell the truth better than one.

LADY. Smart.

PRIMA DONNA. I really see nothing to detain you here now. Good evening Miss . . . er . . . Hewitt.

[*She turns away to her mirror.*

LADY. I'll be going soon. I don't want to upset your grand audience by keeping you.

PRIMA DONNA. Yes. You'd better clear out. I've got to be down on the stage for the beginning of the next scene. The bell's about due. I'm sorry you had to come all this way, Miss Hewitt. I hope you'll find your friend.

LADY. I've found her, Kathie. Kathie . . . [*There is no reply.*] KATHIE . . . [*The Prima Donna arranges her hair.*] Kathie [*deliberately*] do you remember Paul Adams?

PRIMA DONNA [*without turning*]. Paul Adams?

LADY. Yes. You were very sweet on him. A bit too sweet. We in East Street didn't like it.

PRIMA DONNA. I thought you were going?

LADY. You had a crush on Paul Adams. Ruddy soft, you were. Showed feelings your kind wasn't supposed to have . . . [*She comes closer behind the Prima Donna.*] He was killed last week in a motor-bike smash.

PRIMA DONNA [*still without turning*]. Paul Ad . . . Oh, why don't you go?

LADY. Ah! Got you, Kathie! I heard that catch in your throat! I saw your face through the mirror! You thought you were hiding it from me, but I *saw*! Smashed up good and proper was Paul. Died in agony. They say you couldn't recognize his face for blood and mess. Paul's lovely face . . .

and you've kissed it enough . . . Tears in your eyes,
Kathie . . .? Aw, I'm sorry . . . I broke the news a bit sudden.
It fair knocked me up too, though he never meant much to
me.

PRIMA DONNA [*the Italian accent gone*]. Oh, for heaven's sake,
go! Go! [*The bell rings.*

MAID [*jumping up*]. Signorina! The bell!

LADY. Oho! So your hearing has recovered. As quickly
as Kathie's memory.

PRIMA DONNA. Oh Edwards, you fool . . . you fool . . .

MAID. But the bell! Are you ready, Signorina?

LADY. It's all right. I'm off soon. But now all in the garden's
lovely, let's get talking quickly. I've done you good honest
turns in the ol' days, Kathie. What'll you do for me? You're
up in the world of luck, I'm down.

PRIMA DONNA. What do you want?

LADY. I'd keep my mouth shut for . . . five hundred.

PRIMA DONNA. Five hundred!

MAID. Signorina!

LADY. It's worth it to you, I'll bet. You've got a big career
ahead, or so the papers say. I could break it all with my
knowledge. Five hundred'll just keep my tongue locked up.

PRIMA DONNA. You're a dirty swine, Mickey Hewitt; a real
low-down, dirty swine.

LADY. Got the money here? Now?

PRIMA DONNA. No. Unless you will take a cheque. But I
suppose your type must have hard, cold cash.

LADY. I'll manage with a cheque.

[*The Prima Donna goes over to the desk and sits down.*

MAID. But Signorina . . .

PRIMA DONNA. Where on earth is my cheque book,
Edwards?

[*The Maid and the Prima Donna open various drawers,
while the Lady stands in the background.*

MAID. Here it is.

PRIMA DONNA [*quietly*]. You found it too quickly. If only they would start the next scene.

LADY. Hurry, Kathie. I don't want to spoil your evening.

MAID. Oh, you thick-skinned little . . .

PRIMA DONNA [*writing the cheque rather slowly*]. What is a mere evening? It's my whole life you're out to spoil . . . Here's your cheque.

LADY [*coming forward and taking it*]. Thanks. Yes, that seems right. You're the pal you always were.

PRIMA DONNA. I think you're the most despicable rat I ever heard of.

LADY. Now, don't upset everything.

PRIMA DONNA. I hope I never set eyes on you again.

LADY. You won't . . . till I've run through this lot. I've got you now, Kathie. Any nonsense, and I'll split right and left. Keep quiet your end, and it'll be peace at mine. We've both got our work. It's not the same, but we have this little link—the Old Trade Union of East Street. And East Street'll be pretty hot for the next few nights on this little windfall. Why don't you come round and join us? They'll all be proud of you.

PRIMA DONNA. You've got what you want. There's nothing more to be said.

LADY. Yes. I've got it. And pretty smart I've been. I actually had some doubts for a while. You're pretty cleverly made up; I must say I didn't know you from Adam . . . Hm . . . Adam . . . that's what made me certain. Paul Adams . . . The news struck home . . . didn't it?

[*She opens the door and is about to go. Suddenly the music of the next scene of the opera starts up. The Prima Donna smiles broadly at the Maid. The Lady turns back.*]

Hullo . . . I've been keeping you . . .

PRIMA DONNA. The orchestra . . . it's too late . . . I'm ruined!

MAID. Signorina! Hurry!

PRIMA DONNA. It's too late.

LADY. I . . . I didn't mean to.

PRIMA DONNA. You don't care.

LADY. Oh, I do . . .

[*A woman's voice is heard singing in the opera. The Prima Donna and the Maid exchange an obvious glance of triumph. The Lady observes it, and looks from one to the other, puzzled.*

PRIMA DONNA. It's all right, Miss Hewitt. Bianca Marinuzzi reached the stage in time.

LADY. I . . . I don't understand, Bianca . . . 'Ere, what is all this? . . . Oo are you?

PRIMA DONNA. You think you've been smart, Miss Hewitt. But did you *really* suppose Signorina Marinuzzi would be at home to you? Naturally she handed your stupid letter over to us, and left us to deal with you.

LADY. Then . . . Oo are you?

PRIMA DONNA. We are the police.

LADY. The police? Women cops? Gawd!

MAID. Precisely.

PRIMA DONNA. And you've given yourself away nicely. Every word you spoke is down in shorthand.

LADY. No!

MAID [*holding up papers*]. Yes.

PRIMA DONNA. Not so clever after all, Miss Hewitt. First attempt, I should think. And hope, for your sake.

LADY [*after a pause to consider things*]. Well, to think . . . Look here, why did you lead me on? Why didn't you say when I came?

PRIMA DONNA. We wanted to see just how wicked you were. And now we know. Very, very wicked, I'm afraid.

LADY. You led me on. You deliberately tempted me. When you could have warned me and sent me away you sat there and egged me on to say things. Was that fair? I call it damned dirty. You made me ask for that money. Was that honest? Why didn't you just come here in uniform and

K

warn me, instead of all this fancy dress and foolery? Oh, I always knew when they started taking women into the police there'd be some pretty low ideas about the law.

[*She turns again to go.*

PRIMA DONNA. The cheque, please, Miss Hewitt.

LADY. There you are . . . rats!

[*She tears up the cheque, flings it on the floor, and goes out, slamming the door.*

MAID. She left her flowers.

PRIMA DONNA. Policewomen don't usually get bouquets, do they? [*She picks up the torn cheque.*] Paul Adams . . . she as good as had me there . . . Signorina Marinuzzi, your call, please.

QUICK CURTAIN

LADIES-IN-WAITING

by Wendy St John Maule

CHARACTERS

A FAIR VISITOR
A DARK VISITOR
A NURSE
A GIRL
A SISTER
A WOMAN
A GARRULOUS VISITOR

LADIES-IN-WAITING

The action takes place in the waiting-room of a London hospital. It is a cold room, although it is comfortably furnished. The window and the fireplace are L. and R. respectively, the fireplace with a chair above it. The door is facing the audience R., and against the wall and L. of it are two chairs. Across the R. corner is a horsehair sofa. There is a gate-legged table, C., covered with papers and magazines, with two chairs near it, L. and C. respectively.

As the curtain rises the Fair Visitor is sitting on the centre chair near the table, looking at a Tatler. Her friend, the Dark Visitor, is sitting in the chair by the fireplace. They are both well-dressed young women under thirty. A bunch of flowers, a pair of gloves, and a handbag are beside the Fair Visitor's chair.

FAIR VISITOR. I say! Do look at this one!

[*She rises and shows the paper she is reading to the Dark Visitor.*

DARK VISITOR [*reading*]. "Lady Mildred Montague . . ."

FAIR VISITOR. Isn't her hat priceless? How do you think she ever kept it on?

DARK VISITOR [*briefly*]. Elastic. [*Passing it back*] Why people buy hats like that I can't imagine. They can't like wearing them.

FAIR VISITOR. Oh, but they do! I mean, they must, or they wouldn't, would they? [*She returns to table and sits C*

DARK VISITOR. No, I suppose they wouldn't. [*There is a short pause.*] What's the time?

FAIR VISITOR [*looking at her wrist-watch*]. Quarter past three

DARK VISITOR. Good! We'll be allowed in soon.

FAIR VISITOR. I wonder what the baby's like.

148

DARK VISITOR. Like all other babies.

FAIR VISITOR. Oh! But Jane's . . .

DARK VISITOR. It takes true mother-love to know the difference. Jane's, I'm afraid, will be like all the rest, red and squawling. Have you got the flowers?

FAIR VISITOR. Yes, here.

DARK VISITOR. I was afraid you might have left them in the bus. [*She looks round and, rising to her feet, moves behind the table.*] What a dreary place this waiting-room is! If you were dumped in here blindfolded you'd know it was a hospital.

FAIR VISITOR. M-m-m. Sort of smells hospital, doesn't it? You can almost *feel* them operating.

DARK VISITOR [*mockingly, down L.*]. You know, I don't think I'm at all in the right mood to see Jane's baby. One should be full of mother-love, like you, or one can never get the right expression into "Isn't he sweet!" when you really think the child looks like a badly boiled egg.

FAIR VISITOR. Don't you like babies?

DARK VISITOR. I consider them messy and unhygienic.

FAIR VISITOR [*protesting*]. But, darling . . .!

DARK VISITOR. Well, you can't deny it, can you?

FAIR VISITOR. N-no; but some are rather sweet.

DARK VISITOR. I'm afraid I've got no maternal instincts. [*There are footsteps off.*] Thank God! Let's hope that's for us.

> [*The door opens and a Nurse shows in the Girl. She is small and fair, about twenty-two years old, and is neatly but not expensively dressed. She is obviously desperately worried and on the verge of tears.*

NURSE. If you'll wait in here, madam, I'll call you when Mr Wright is through. Mrs Richards, isn't it?

GIRL [*after the slightest pause*]. Yes.

> [*She goes and sits by the fireplace.*

DARK VISITOR. Can we see Mrs Cartwright yet?

NURSE. I'll go and inquire. [*Exit the Nurse.*

DARK VISITOR [*sitting on the sofa*]. How sickening! Now I

suppose we wait for another half-hour. Pass me over *Punch*, will you? [*Fair Visitor does so.*] No, not that one—the other.

FAIR VISITOR. This?

DARK VISITOR. Yes. Thanks.

[*There is silence for a few minutes. The Girl by the fire is clutching and unclutching a handkerchief. She seems oblivious of all around her. Then the Fair Visitor looks up, looks at the table and under the chair.*

FAIR VISITOR [*in a tone of agony*]. Chris!

DARK VISITOR [*still reading*]. U-u-m?

FAIR VISITOR. Chris, I've lost my bag! [*She gets up and peers round the room.*] I must have left it in the bus!

DARK VISITOR [*looking up lazily*]. Did you ever have anything you didn't lose?

FAIR VISITOR [*racking her brains*]. I know I had it in my hand when I got on to the bus, and then——

DARK VISITOR. Isn't that it by the flowers?

[*The Fair Visitor removes the flowers, and there lies the bag.*

FAIR VISITOR. So it is! How silly of me!

[*Enter the Nurse.*

NURSE. Mrs Cartwright can see you now.

DARK VISITOR [*rising and going to the door, followed by the Fair Visitor, clutching her bag and gloves*]. Now you haven't got the flowers.

FAIR VISITOR. Heavens, I nearly forgot them!

[*She goes back and gets them, and in doing so drops the gloves on the table. They go out.*

NURSE [*at the door*]. Nurse Howard! Will you show these ladies to Room 102?

[*She re-enters, crosses to the table, and tidies the papers.*

GIRL. How long do you think it will be before I can see my —[*she pauses ever so slightly*] my husband?

NURSE. About twenty minutes. Mr Wright hasn't finished operating yet.

GIRL [*tears thick in her voice*]. D'you think there's a chance?

NURSE [*briskly*]. Of course there's a chance. Mr Wright is a wonderful surgeon. [*The Girl says nothing.*] You mustn't worry. We don't want another patient on our hands, do we? Here's a new *Tatler*. Have you seen it?

GIRL [*listlessly*]. No.

NURSE [*going to her*]. Here you are, then, and I'll come back for you in about twenty minutes. [*She goes towards the door.*] Would you like a nice cup of tea?

GIRL. Tea? No, thank you.

NURSE. Nothing I can get you?

GIRL. No, thank you.

NURSE. I'll be back just as soon as you can see him.

GIRL. Thank you.

[*Exit the Nurse. The Girl sits staring straight in front of her. She looks at her watch, and then rises and goes to the window R. and looks out. The* Tatler *falls unheeded to the floor. There are footsteps off, and the Sister enters. She ushers in the Woman, whose age might be anything from thirty-five to forty-five. She is dressed in black, and her clothes are obviously expensive.*]

SISTER. Will you wait in here, please? [*The Woman goes to the table C.*] The doctor should be finished any moment now. [*She sees the* Tatler, *picks it up, and places it on the table. The Woman has taken off her gloves and places them, with her bag, on top of those belonging to the Fair Visitor.*] Is there anything I can get you after your long journey?

WOMAN. No, thank you. I had lunch on the boat.

SISTER. I'll come and fetch you when they're ready.

WOMAN. Thank you, Sister. [*Exit the Sister. The Woman idly picks up a paper, but is stopped short by the sound of a stifled sob from the Girl, who has her back to her.*] Is there anything I can do?

GIRL [*between tears*]. No, thank you. Nothing.

WOMAN [*gently*]. You're sure?

GIRL. Absolutely. [*Turning*] I'm sorry. I'm making a fool of myself.

WOMAN [*going to her*]. We all do that at times. [*She takes her gently by the shoulder.*] Come and sit down. [*She leads her to the sofa, sitting on the right of her.*] Have you got much longer to wait? [*The Girl shakes her head.*] Are you sure there's nothing I can do?

GIRL. Nothing . . . I'm sorry. It's the waiting gets on my nerves.

WOMAN. Waiting's the worst part. [*The Girl nods, drying her eyes.*] When the good news comes you'll forget that you had to wait.

GIRL. When it comes . . . If it comes . . .

WOMAN. Afraid?

GIRL. Horribly.

WOMAN. Don't think about it too much. Thinking makes it worse.

GIRL. I know, but it's the whole atmosphere of this place: so cold, so white, so—so—inhuman! And somewhere in the middle of it all they're hurting him, and I can do nothing —nothing! Only sit here . . .

WOMAN. He's very ill?

GIRL. Yes. This operation's the only chance. [*She rises and walks R.*] It mustn't fail! It mustn't! It mustn't! [*Going back to the Woman.*] You must think me mad.

WOMAN. No, my dear.

GIRL. But if you knew what it meant to me . . . [*Sitting L. of table.*] And this awful waiting . . .

WOMAN [*rising, a hand on the Girl's shoulder*]. You love him so very much?

GIRL. More than anything in the world. Forgive me, but I've been nearly worried to death. And I've had no one to talk to, no one I could talk to. It's so awful when everything gets bottled up inside, you know.

WOMAN [*sitting C.*]. Yes.

GIRL. And when you're by yourself little things and worries add up, until you think you'll go insane!

WOMAN. I know. I've been through it myself.

GIRL. You know what it's like, this—this——

WOMAN [*quietly*]. Yes, I'm waiting now.

GIRL. You?

WOMAN. Yes. And for someone I love very much: my husband.

GIRL. You make me feel so ashamed.

WOMAN. Why? I'm older than you.

GIRL. What difference does that make?

WOMAN. I think when one is older things don't go so deep. One feels them just the same, but without the intensity of youth. You see, we've had our good times and our bad, and we see things in better perspective.

GIRL. Perhaps that's true. I've never had a good time, not really good. And just when it was beginning this happened. Sometimes I think I am fated with ill luck.

WOMAN. As long as you can keep love you can fight even Fate. It's when you lose it . . .

GIRL. You think that?

WOMAN. I know it. Listen! Even if your husband dies [*the Girl catches her breath*] your love for him and his for you will still remain. Won't it?

GIRL. I suppose so.

WOMAN. But if you live to grow old you'll live to see that love fade and wither away. If it should be broken now you'll have it always.

GIRL [*passionately*]. I'd rather have him always!

WOMAN. Without his love?

GIRL. But that wouldn't change!

WOMAN. It might.

GIRL [*turning on her*]. Oh, you don't understand! We're—we're different! I mean everything to him, and he's all the world to me!

WOMAN. You think so now. When I married I thought that too, but—these last two years—everything's different. Time alters things so.

GIRL. It couldn't alter our love!

WOMAN. You're very sure.

GIRL [*rising and gazing at the door*]. I have to be sure! [*Moving R.*] He's all I've got to love, and without him—I couldn't go on without him; it wouldn't be possible! Not if you're like me, and— [*Her voice changes.*] I'm afraid I'm making a fool of myself again.

> [*She stops as she hears footsteps, and turns eagerly to the door, which is opened by the Sister. The Fair Visitor bursts in. The Girl turns back and sits R., disappointed. The Dark Visitor follows her friend, looking distinctly bored.*

FAIR VISITOR [*talking agitatedly over her shoulder to the Dark Visitor*]. I know I had them a minute ago. They were in my hand when you asked me had I got the flowers. [*As she is talking she is peering round the room and under the furniture. The Dark Visitor remains with the Sister by the door.*] They were a new pair, too. I only got them three days ago. It really is too bad.

DARK VISITOR [*mockingly*]. Thank heaven Jane had the baby and not you!

FAIR VISITOR [*down L.*]. Why?

DARK VISITOR. Had it been your baby you'd have lost it immediately.

FAIR VISITOR [*on her knees by sofa, L.*]. Being a spinster, I should think that rather lucky.

WOMAN [*removing her bag and picking up the gloves*]. Are these what you're looking for?

FAIR VISITOR [*darting at them*]. Oh, yes! [*Taking them up*] Thank you, so much! [*Moving up R.*] Thanks awfully! [*Going to the door*] I knew I had them in my hand when I came into the room. I must have dropped them.

DARK VISITOR [*as the Fair Visitor goes out; dryly*]. Yes, you must have dropped them. [*As she follows her*] How you ever have anything left to lose . . .

> [*Her voice dies away down the corridor. The Sister shuts the door.*

GIRL. Oh, why don't they come?

WOMAN [*soothing her*]. They'll come soon.

GIRL. If only I could be certain it would be successful! But I know somehow—Oh, I can't explain!

WOMAN. You mustn't worry so much. Your husband will be all right.

GIRL. I don't know why you're being so kind to me. You ought to curse me for a silly fool.

WOMAN. Nonsense!

GIRL. Besides—[*with a rush*] I told you a lie when I said he was my husband. He's not. [*There is a pause.*] You're shocked?

WOMAN. I? No.

GIRL. So, you see, I've got no right to be here at all. The hospital think I'm his wife. I was forced to say that because I had to see him. But he's married to someone else. That's why I've had no one to talk to, no one whose advice I could ask. No one knows about—about us. We were going away together when this happened. [*Rising and standing R.*] God knows why I'm telling you all this! But I've kept everything secret for so long I must tell somebody!

WOMAN. Go on. I think I understand.

GIRL. It all started quite casually—until we found we loved each other. Oh, please don't think it was just a passing *affaire*. It wasn't: it was the real thing. His wife is older than he is, and I don't think he ever really loved her.

WOMAN. He may have done.

GIRL. Anyway, we decided to go away together—it was no good asking her for a divorce: she's a Catholic; and then the day before we were leaving Mark fell ill.

WOMAN [*in a strangled voice*]. Mark!

GIRL [*not noticing*]. So everything was over.

WOMAN. You said his name was Mark?

GIRL. I shouldn't have told you that, should I? But it just slipped out.

[*She is too preoccupied with her own troubles to notice any-one else's.*

WOMAN. And his wife's a Catholic?

GIRL. Yes. That was why, you see, it was no good telling her. He wanted to, but——

[*She stops as she hears footsteps off. The Woman has gone as pale as death.*

[*Enter the Nurse. The Girl starts to her feet.*

NURSE [*to Girl*]. Mr Wright is not quite through yet.

[*The Girl goes to the sofa L. and sits down. Enter the Garrulous Visitor, a short, stout, shabby woman, clutching an enormous handbag. Her grey hair is untidy, and we strongly suspect her of wearing elastic-sided boots.*

Will you wait in here, please?

GARRULOUS VISITOR [*with a distinct Cockney accent*]. Is Willie any better, Nurse?

NURSE. I haven't seen him to-day.

GARRULOUS VISITOR. Can I see 'im soon?

NURSE. I am just going to inquire.

[*She goes out. The Garrulous Visitor seats herself comfort-ably on the chair L. of the door.*

GARRULOUS VISITOR [*looking round*]. I 'ates this waitin', don't you? [*No one answers her.*] Sort of gets on your nerves like, don't it. [*There is silence.*

WOMAN [*realizing she expects an answer*]. Yes.

GARRULOUS VISITOR. I always sez to my old man, "The part I 'ates," I sez, "is waitin' before they'll let me see my Willie." [*Rising and coming R. of the Woman*] "'Ow do I know," I sez, "they won't 'ave changed their minds and cut 'im up again durin' the night?" [*Sitting R.*] And yer can't get any change out of them nurses, can yer? [*There is no answer, but *this does not worry her.*] But I s'pose when yer sees illness and sufferin' all round yer yer gets 'ardened like. Treats 'em like numbers, they do; not that I don't say they treats 'em well. [*There is a pause.*] D'you know, the day I brought my Willie in 'ere, 'is leg bleedin' somethin' awful, they were as cheerful as though it were a picnic. A bloomin' lot too cheerful, as I told my old man. Like as though they enjoyed 'im bein' ill——

GIRL [*rising and turning on her*]. Oh, be quiet, can't you?

GARRULOUS VISITOR. Well! I'll be——

GIRL [*turning away*]. I'm sorry.

GARRULOUS VISITOR. And so I should 'ope! World's a free place, I believe.

WOMAN. Her—her husband is very ill.

GARRULOUS VISITOR. I'm sorry. But 'ow was I to know a little conversation wouldn't sort of . . . [*Her voice tails away.*] I'm sorry, I'm sure. [*She sits fiddling with her bag. The Girl goes to the window, R., her back to the room.*] I'd be the last to intrude when not wanted.

> [*There is silence for a short time. Then the Nurse's footsteps are heard in the passage outside. The Girl turns eagerly. The door opens and the Nurse enters.*

NURSE. Mrs Walker, Willie's ready now.

> [*The Girl turns back, disappointed.*

GARRULOUS VISITOR [*rising*]. Thank you, Nurse. [*To Girl*] I'm sorry. [*Going R. of chair*] Reely I am. [*The Girl takes no notice.*] But 'ow was I to know, I asks yer, 'ow was I to know? [*As she goes through the door*] Which way did yer say? . . . Up 'ere?   [*Her voice dies away down the passage.*

GIRL [*turning to the Nurse*]. Will they be through soon?

NURSE. I think so. I'll come the moment they are.

> [*She goes out, shutting the door behind her. The Girl goes to the table, and stands aimlessly turning over the papers; then sits in the chair L., her head in her hands.*

GIRL. God! Oh, God!

WOMAN [*rising and moving L. and speaking in a flat, impersonal voice*]. Tell me, what will you do if your—friend does get well?

GIRL. Do? Begin to live again, I suppose.

WOMAN [*in a quiet, dead voice*]. You've known your friend long?

GIRL. About two years.

WOMAN [*half to herself*]. Two years . . .

GIRL. We couldn't see each other often. It was a furtive, underhand business; it had to be. But when we could meet it was paradise.

WOMAN. Paradise!

GIRL. I didn't know it was possible for two people to be so happy. It was as though someone had opened the doors of a prison for me.

WOMAN [*turning towards the Girl*]. And the wife?

GIRL. She's in France. She doesn't know yet—about his being ill, I mean. I've never seen her. [*The Woman turns away.*] I expect you think me awful, don't you? We tried so hard to be straightforward and honourable about it, but it just couldn't be done. We couldn't part: it wasn't possible. But now this place has done what we couldn't do.

WOMAN. Will you go away with him? If he gets well, that is.

GIRL [*simply*]. Yes. [*Fiercely*] I daren't think of it—daren't!

WOMAN [*with great effort*]. You don't think he'll ever regret his wife, or leave you as he is leaving her?

GIRL [*with complete conviction*]. No. He loves me.

WOMAN. He may have thought once he loved her.

GIRL. Not as he loves me. No, we'll sail away, away, and live happy ever after!

WOMAN. You're very sure of happiness.

GIRL [*turning a radiant face to her*]. If you knew him you wouldn't doubt it. No one could be unhappy whom he loved.

WOMAN. And you don't feel jealous of his wife.

GIRL. If he cared for her—yes, I should feel jealous. As it is, I only grudge her the time that she has had with him, and I grudge her every minute of that. But I'm not jealous of her, only desperately sorry.

WOMAN. Then you have thought of her?

GIRL. Sometimes until my head was nearly bursting. It seemed such a mean, dirty trick, and I know if I had him and lost him how I should feel. But how can I leave him when it's me he loves? [*The Woman turns away.*] I am robbing her of nothing, for his love had already gone. I should only be leaving her the husk of things.

WOMAN [*sitting R.*]. She might treasure even that. Women do, you know.

GIRL [*rising and crossing to her*]. How can I give her what I need so desperately myself?

WOMAN. I don't know.

GIRL. Mark was so sure that it was the only thing to do, that it was the thing that would hurt her least. We couldn't go on as we were, always inventing excuses and lies to meet, and we couldn't part. There was nothing else we could do.

WOMAN. No, I suppose not. [*Almost to herself*] At least, she has her memories, poor as they are.

GIRL. You talk as if you knew her.

WOMAN [*hastily, almost too hastily*]. I? How could I? But I do know what it's like to love someone, and to see their love for you slipping each day a little farther beyond your reach, until one day it has all quite gone. So, you see, I'm sorry for her.

GIRL. You must think me hard.

WOMAN. No. [*Rising and facing her*] We must each get what we can out of life. You know what you want, and you're going for it. I wish my own objective was as plain.

GIRL. Am I wrong, d'you think? I mean, d'you think I ought to give him up?

WOMAN. That rests with your own self and with him.

GIRL [*going C.*]. I couldn't give him up! He's so much part of me. I couldn't do it!

WOMAN. That is nearer the truth.

GIRL [*turning to her*]. Oh, I know you think I'm wicked and hard and selfish! And you're right: I am! But I've had so little out of life, and now I've got something at last I mean to hang on to it. God can't have given him to me just to snatch him away again!

WOMAN. It might be better like that.

GIRL. What do you mean?

WOMAN. You might destroy your happiness and save your soul.

GIRL. You're religious?

WOMAN. Yes.

GIRL. I'm not. If I were I wouldn't be here. But when something happens to you as big as this you're above priests and conventional laws.

WOMAN. But can you remain above them? Won't they pull you down in the end?

GIRL. Not when your love is as strong as ours. [*Going to her*] What can be wrong in stealing a little happiness? Heaven knows, we see little enough of it.

WOMAN [*moving up C.*]. Happiness is such an elusive thing that even as we hold it it has gone. [*Coming down L.*] And if you climb to it on other people's shoulders the time will come when you yourself are the rung in someone else's ladder.

GIRL. I wouldn't care!

WOMAN [*moving towards her*]. Are you so sure?

GIRL. If I'd had my happiness I wouldn't mind paying for it. That's only fair.

WOMAN. Perhaps you are paying for some of it now. If you didn't love him you wouldn't be unhappy, would you?

GIRL [*slowly*]. No . . . But it's been worth it! Terribly worth it!

WOMAN [*going to her, her back to the audience*]. You mean that?

GIRL. Every word of it! I'd go through this again and again if only to see him once!

WOMAN [*almost sorrowfully*]. Then you really love him?

GIRL [*her face radiant*]. Do you doubt it?

WOMAN [*moving down L.*]. No, I don't.

[*Enter the Nurse. The Girl turns expectantly.*

NURSE. Mrs Richards. [*The Girl goes over to her quickly, The Woman inadvertently turns on hearing her name, and for one split second she seems to be making a decision. Then she turns slowly back.*] Will you come this way, Mrs Richards? Your husband can see you now.

GIRL. Has it . . .? Is it a success?

NURSE [*smiling*]. Yes. Complete.

GIRL [*almost overcome*]. Thank God! [*Recovering herself*] Which way do I go? . . . Here?

[*She goes out, the Nurse following her.*

NURSE [*off*]. Nurse Howard! Show Mrs Richards to Room 80.

[*During this the Woman has been staring straight in front of her, her hands alone betraying her emotion. The Nurse re-enters.*

[*Coming down behind the table*] You were waiting to see somebody?

WOMAN [*struggling to regain composure*]. I? Oh, yes . . . Yes . . . But I don't think I'll stay now. [*She moves to table and picks up her gloves.*] I—I—have another engagement. [*She goes to the door, but turns in the doorway.*] Tell me, will her husband recover?

NURSE. There is every chance of it.

WOMAN. Thank you. That was all I wanted to know.

[*She goes out as the curtain falls.*

NO TEARS FOR HENRY

A COMEDY FOR FIVE WOMEN

by Winifred Bannister

CHARACTERS

MRS MARSDEN, *mother*
ANNA, *her maid*
JANE
HENRIETTA } *her daughters*
MARIAN LORNE, *doctor*

SCENE: The lounge of a provincial house

TIME: The present; about 4 P.M.

NO TEARS FOR HENRY

Mrs Marsden, a well-preserved woman of sixty-five, is arranging red roses in her lounge. The old lady's smile suggests that there is some secret shared by herself and the roses. The room is comfortably furnished. There is a settee beside the French window, R., and a small table before this. The hall door is in the L. corner. There is a photograph of Henry, Mrs Marsden's deceased husband, on the back wall. On the settee is a knitting-bag and a newspaper. Mrs Marsden turns as Anna, her elderly servant, enters, carrying a white iced cake, decorated with cherries.

MRS MARSDEN. Oh, Anna!   [*Anna approaches table.*

ANNA. A wee birthday present, ma'am. It's no verra much, but I thocht it might give ye a bit of a pairty feeling.

MRS MARSDEN. It does give me a party feeling, Anna. It looks so very festive. Let me put it beside the flowers. It seems to belong, doesn't it? You have been very clever keeping it secret.

ANNA [*beaming*]. There now, ma'am, ye dinna ken what goes on in your ain kitchen.

MRS MARSDEN. Neither I do, Anna. I'm afraid I have always left you very much on your own.

ANNA. That's a thing I've aye liked ye for, ma'am. Ye've aye trustit me and treated me mair like your ain sister than a servant.

MRS MARSDEN. Well, I'm glad you have been happy here, Anna. You have always been an easy person to trust.

ANNA. Thank you, ma'am. [*Looking at cake*] I hope ye'll no' feel the cherries an extravagance. The master was sae fond o' them, and I felt ye'd like things just as usual even though he——   [*She stops, wondering if she has said too much.*

MRS MARSDEN. Even though the master isn't here, you were going to say, Anna. But he is here! Look at these roses from his hothouse.

ANNA. Aye, the master was terrible fond of his roses, and there has aye been a dozen red yins for your birthday. It was the first thing he did. He'd be doon the stair like a lad and intae the greenhouse, and when I came in tae lay the table, there they'd be, looking that bonny o' the white cloth, just as I found them the morn——

MRS MARSDEN [*sharply*]. You *found* them like that this morning?

ANNA. Aye, ma'am, I thocht ye'd picked them.

MRS MARSDEN [*shaking her head*]. No, Anna, I thought it was you; I took it for granted it was you.

ANNA [*clapping a hand to her mouth*]. Guid sakes! Wha then? [*She suddenly relaxes as a thought strikes her.*] Och, of course, it was the gairdner. Aye, it must hae been. He's a dour body, but awfu' soft hairted. I'll ask him.

MRS MARSDEN [*quickly*]. No, Anna, don't ask him. Leave it alone. It doesn't matter; they are there as Henry meant them to be. [*Pause.*

ANNA [*slowly*]. As ye wish, ma'am. [*She nervously clasps and unclasps her hands as though struggling with her thoughts.*] Ma'am?

MRS MARSDEN. Yes, Anna, what is it?

ANNA. I hope ye'll no' mind me taking the liberty, ma'am, but I've been kinda worrit aboot ye. [*Mrs Marsden raises an eyebrow.*] Throwing off your blacks and dressing yoursel' in colours. Mind ye, it was a relief tae hear ye singing again, and tae see ye back tae your cheery self, but it seemed kinda unnatural after ye nearly killt yourself wi' fretting for the first month or two.

MRS MARSDEN [*slowly*]. Yes, Anna, I suppose it did seem odd. But you see, I had reached a depth of misery not to be borne, and quite suddenly I felt ashamed.

ANNA [*surprised*]. Ashamed, ma'am?

MRS MARSDEN. Yes; that after forty years of happiness with my husband I could hold on to so little of it that I wept my eyes dry as soon as he had gone. In a flash it came to me as I was searching for a way out of my despair that if I could only accept Henry's death calmly I could bring him back.

ANNA [*horrified*]. Bring him back! Losh me, that's a thing naebody can dae—bring the deid back to life.

MRS MARSDEN. Well, of course, I don't mean bring him back in the flesh, Anna.

ANNA. Mercy me, but we want nae spirits! I shouldna sleep a wink if I thocht the master was haunting us.

MRS MARSDEN. There is no ghost, Anna.

[*She picks up her knitting from settee, but merely holds it.*

ANNA [*baffled*]. Weel, if there's nae flesh and nae spirit, ma'am, what is there tae a human body?

MRS MARSDEN. It's difficult to explain. It is just something that exists in the mind. Nothing more than what memory and make-believe can create.

ANNA. It sounds awfu' like a fairy tale tae me, ma'am, but maybe it's no' a bad thing. It wouldna be the first time a broken heart had been cured wi' a fairy tale. Aye, and it's queer like ye should say that aboot bringing the master back. I [*she pauses and almost whispers, head bent forward*] have felt him aboot the hoose.

MRS MARSDEN. Ah! You feel it too, Anna?

ANNA. Aye, when I was hanging oot the claes yesterday I thocht I saw the master's heid bobbing up and doon the hedge as he worked in the gairden. An' I shouldna be surprised tae hear him say any morning like he used: "Weel, Joanna, how are your bunions this morning?"

MRS MARSDEN [*laughing and starting to knit slowly*]. Perhaps we are both mad, Anna. I saw him at breakfast this morning frowning over the news and fingering his tie—such a threadbare one. You know how he would stick to one tie. [*Anna nods, smiling.*] And I actually made a mental note: "Buy Henry a new tie."

ANNA [*her eyes opening wide*]. But ye willna dae that, ma'am?

MRS MARSDEN. Of course not, Anna. But you see he does pop up now and then as though he were still alive. There's nothing supernatural about it. At our age, perhaps, memories are so real that they can push out reality.

ANNA. Aye, I ken fine what you mean, ma'am. But will it last? That's what I'm feart on—that it micht be like yin o' yon owerbright morns, that end wi' rain coming doon i' buckets.

MRS MARSDEN. I don't think so, Anna. You see, out of my fairy story, as you call it, I'm going to build something solid enough for a Lord Mayor to open.

ANNA (*flabbergasted*). Solid—enough—for—a—Lord—Mayor—tae—open! [*Light dawning*] Dae ye mean a kind o' memorial?

MRS MARSDEN. Well, yes—though I hadn't thought of it as that. I'm turning my Sussex property—Great Beeches—into small comfortable flats for old widows who have not only lost their husbands, but who have to suffer poverty too.

ANNA [*beaming*]. And is that no' a grand idea! Ye've been coonting your blessings and finding there were others a lot worse off than yoursel'. Aye, that maks sense a' recht.

MRS MARSDEN [*puts down knitting*]. Yes, I have been counting my blessings, Anna. I've got the whole thing planned. Workmen are in Great Beeches now, and when I have sold this house I shall go down there.

ANNA [*sadly*]. Dae ye mean ye'll be living wi' the auld ladies, ma'am?

MRS MARSDEN. Yes, though of course I shall have my own little flat.

ANNA [*sadly*]. Then ye'll no' need me, ma'am.

MRS MARSDEN. But I should like you to come, Anna. I

thought you might feel the time had come for you to have a change.

ANNA [*happy again*]. Na, I couldnae leave ye noo after a' these years, and how dae ye think ye could manage a bunch o' grannies wi'oot me? They'd have ye in the madhouse wi' their queer notions. I mind ma auld Aunt Essie. She wouldna gang on a visit wi'oot her clocks; three o' they cuckoo clocks, all striking at different times. She had us a' fair dementit nicht and day wi' her cuckoos.

MRS MARSDEN. Oh, there will be a few eccentrics, I've no doubt. But what does it matter? When we grow old we are all a little mad. I shall employ some kind, middle-aged woman to act as a sort of matron. The rough work is to be done by charwomen, and I hoped that you would keep them in order for me and manage the kitchen staff, Anna.

ANNA. I will that, ma'am.

MRS MARSDEN. That is settled, then. My job will be to supervise the garden. We shall grow everything we can.

ANNA. My, I'm fair excited aboot it! There's ma daughter Jean wanting me tae gang and live wi' her because she thinks I'm in ma dotage and fit for nae mair than pushing a pram roon the Botanic Gairdens, and there's your daughters thinking it's time ye settled doon in a corner wi' your knitting. Aye, but they've a' got the wrang soo by the lug!

MRS MARSDEN [*laughing*]. Yes, Anna, we'll show them. Good gracious! [*as she looks at the clock*] the girls will be here any minute. Another committee meeting, I've no doubt. I wish they wouldn't; they make me feel like an institution.

ANNA. Aye, they're awfu' guid at that. [*As she goes towards door*] I'll gang and put the kettle on. [*Turning to face Mrs Marsden*] But for the guid Lord's sake, ma'am, dinna buy a new tie for the master, or I shall ken that yin o' us is wrang in the heid!

[*Exit Anna. A bell rings as she goes out. Mrs Marsden picks*

*up her knitting, then suddenly puts it down as she remembers
there is something she wishes to see in the newspaper beside
her. She looks at this, but puts it down as Henrietta and Jane,
her two daughters, enter. Both are in deep mourning.
Henrietta is a nervous, restless creature with too much
imagination. Jane, who has too little, has a firm and business-
like grasp of life, which her family would willingly exchange
for a little lovingkindness.*

HENRIETTA. Many happy returns, Mother.   [*They kiss.*

MRS MARSDEN. Thank you, Henrietta.

JANE. Happy birthday, Mother. [*They kiss. Jane hands over
two parcels.*] Here are our presents, Mother. The soft one is
from Edward. He couldn't come at the last minute; he had a
directors' meeting.

MRS MARSDEN. Oh, he had, had he? Edward has as many
directors' meetings as most people have grandmothers. I'm
not too old to be excited at the sight of a parcel. [*Opening the
soft one*] I know what Edward's will be. [*She pulls out a hot-
water bottle wearing a fluffy cover.*] The usual hot-water bottle,
but he has excelled himself this time; a nice fluffy cover to
keep my poor senile feet from burning.

[*Henrietta and Jane exchange a look.*

JANE. I expect Edward wanted to give you something
really useful. After all, you don't want fripperies at your age,
do you now, Mother?

MRS MARSDEN. Even in my *decrepit* old age, Jane, I shall like
pretty things as much as I ever did. [*She turns to the other
parcel.*] Ah—[*with genuine delight*] a dear little stone vase for
my garden. Now, that is original of you.

HENRIETTA. It is really intended for Father's grave, Mother.
We thought it badly needed something of the kind; it is quite
the dullest in his row.

JANE [*severely*]. And certainly the untidiest.

MRS MARSDEN. So you thought you would encourage me to
doll it up with flowers!

HENRIETTA. "Doll it up," Mother! That is hardly the way to put it.

> [*Mrs Marsden begins to laugh and in a few minutes is consumed with mirth. Henrietta and Jane preserve a dignified silence.*

MRS MARSDEN. Oh dear, forgive me, you are so solemn and funny. Henry would be amused——

JANE [*breaking in*]. There is nothing funny about showing respect to the dead, Mother.

MRS MARSDEN. Remembering the patch of earth containing Henry's bones, my dear Jane, is not remembering Henry. If you want this thing on the grave, you had better take it yourself. I never go near the place; to me it is dead and empty.

HENRIETTA. Well really, Mother, what do you expect in a cemetery?

MRS MARSDEN [*irritably*]. I expect nothing; that is why I never go. Now you have depressed me. All these black clothes you are wearing. With your complexion, Henrietta, you should never wear black.

HENRIETTA. I am not wearing black, Mother, because I like it, but out of respect for poor Father.

JANE. And while we are on the subject, Mother, I must say that I think you might at least wear black in public. After all, it is less than six months since Father died; people are talking.

MRS MARSDEN. Henry hates black, he always did. His funeral, he said, was quite his dullest experience.

JANE. What—what was that you said, Mother?

HENRIETTA [*on a high note*]. D-did you say—do you mean that Father was at his own funeral?

MRS MARSDEN. Well, of course, Henrietta; how could a dead man not be present at his own funeral?

JANE. Mother, you are rambling!

HENRIETTA [*fearfully*]. Do you mean that Father w-walks?

JANE [*impatiently*]. Don't be silly, Henrietta. Really,

Mother, I'm surprised at you, dabbling in Spiritualism. It will not bring Father back to you.

MRS MARSDEN. There is no ism about it, Jane. It is quite simple. From long habit, your father is still with me. In the first shock of grief I did not realize this, but once I could talk with him again, it was as if he had never been away.

HENRIETTA [*who, from now on, cannot rid herself of the feeling that a ghost looks over her shoulder*]. *Talk* with him! Oh, Mother! you don't mean that he comes to you in the night?

MRS MARSDEN. Well, he doesn't behave like the average ghost, Henrietta, but does sometimes say——

HENRIETTA [*horribly fascinated*]. Yes, Mother?

MRS MARSDEN. "Must you stick your knees in the middle of my back, Emily?"

JANE. I've heard enough of this. It's disgraceful, Mother. Disgraceful or pathetic.

MRS MARSDEN. I prefer disgraceful.

JANE. You must be ill—you can't know what you are saying.

HENRIETTA. Oh, my poor unhappy mother.

MRS MARSDEN. Unhappy fiddlesticks. I have not felt so well and happy for months.

HENRIETTA. Poor Father. He would turn in his grave if he could hear you.

MRS MARSDEN. How Henry hates that old wives' refrain! He said only the other day, "For God's sake, Emily, stop them saying that; it's macabre."

JANE. Mother, if this is a joke you are playing on us, it is in very bad taste. It's shocking to treat death so flippantly.

MRS MARSDEN. I'm not being flippant, Jane. I am making the best of what death has dealt to me. That is not being flippant; it's being resourceful.

HENRIETTA. But you will never have any peace, Mother, if you don't let the dead rest.

MRS MARSDEN. Will you stop talking about the dead, Henrietta? Such morbidity—on my birthday, too. For heaven's sake, Jane, ring the bell for Anna. Let's have some tea and get the taste of death out of our mouths.

HENRIETTA [*dramatically*]. *Tea*, Mother, *tea*! It would choke me. I think I'll go into the garden and pick a few flowers for Father's grave.

MRS MARSDEN [*as Henrietta makes for the garden door*]. There she goes again with her talk of graves! Your father doesn't want any flowers on his grave, Henrietta; he prefers to see them in the garden where he planted them.

[*With a sob, Henrietta goes out into the garden.*]
Poor Henrietta, she was always inclined to be hysterical.

[*Anna enters with tea-tray.*
ANNA. Will I pour out, ma'am, or will you?

MRS MARSDEN. Just take Miss Henrietta some tea, Anna, will you? If we don't give her some occupation while she is in the garden, I am afraid she will pick all Henry's favourite roses.

[*There is a short scream from the direction of the garden.*]
I expect she has seen the gardener in that old Panama of her father's; she is determined to go home with a ghost.

ANNA [*as she goes out with tea*]. It's no' tea she's needing, but a bucket o' cold water!

JANE [*to her mother*]. Henrietta will go home with a ghost all right. We shall be the laughing stock of the place. Quite frankly, Mother, I'm disgusted with you. The proper place for the dead is the grave. If you want to keep your sanity you had better reconcile yourself soon to Father's death.

MRS MARSDEN [*cutting cake*]. Have a piece of this delicious cake. Wasn't it thoughtful of Anna to put the cherries on for Henry?

JANE [*with a heavy sigh*]. Just a small piece. Is Anna in this too? It seems to me that I am the only sane body in the house. I have come to the conclusion that you had better make your home with us, Mother. We can make room for you; Nanny is leaving soon.

MRS MARSDEN. Then engage another, Jane. I know you have all been making plans for me to stay with each of you in turn, but I don't want to bob about like a commercial traveller.

JANE. But surely, Mother, the obvious thing to do is to sell your property and settle down with us.

MRS MARSDEN. If you want any fun out of life, Jane, avoid the obvious.

JANE [really angry]. Fun, Mother? Haven't you got fun on the brain? You make fun of Father's death, fun of my efforts to arrange your old age——

MRS MARSDEN [breaking in]. And why shouldn't I? What with one daughter who talks tombs, and another who sticks a little lace cap on my head, do you wonder I introduce a little comic relief. As for my *old age*, Jane, I have my own plans. I am going to live at Great Beeches.

JANE. What? That great barn of a house!

MRS MARSDEN. It isn't a great barn any longer. It is being converted into the most charming little flats.

JANE. Flats? So that is where all your money has been going. Well, of course, it might be a good investment.

MRS MARSDEN. A very good investment. I shall get a lot of pleasure out of it.

JANE. Pleasure? You mean money, surely?

MRS MARSDEN. No, merely pleasure. You see, the flats will be occupied by old ladies with small incomes.

JANE. You mean rent free?

MRS MARSDEN. Yes. I am selling this property and shall live in one of the flats myself—the one overlooking Henry's rockery.

JANE. It's sheer madness. *Giving* your property away. Why, you'll be penniless.

MRS MARSDEN. I shall have enough. Has it ever struck you,

Jane, that when somebody gives something for something, it is considered right and natural. I once heard a diplomat call it "justifiable self-interest." But when one gives something for nothing—then it is madness. No wonder the world is full of conflict.

[*Enter Henrietta, looking like a tragedy queen. She carries a bunch of white flowers.*]

Well, Henrietta, I hope you are feeling sufficiently robust to hear that I have been giving away some of my property.

HENRIETTA [*coming to life*]. What's this?

JANE. Mother is turning Great Beeches into an institution for old women.

HENRIETTA [*throwing down flowers on to her chair*]. Old women! But what about us? It's preposterous. You can't afford such philanthropy, Mother.

MRS MARSDEN. I am the best judge of that, Henrietta.

HENRIETTA. Haven't you ever heard that charity begins at home?

MRS MARSDEN. I have never thought much of charity in or out of the home.

JANE. Well, has it occurred to you that if you squander your money, you make yourself dependent on us?

MRS MARSDEN. Ah, there's the rub.

JANE. And why not? Father meant us to benefit after you; not a lot of old charwomen. [*Enter Anna.*

ANNA. There's a sharp-voiced body on the phone, ma'am. She says it's about the advertisement in the paper.

MRS MARSDEN [*rising*]. Oh yes, Anna, I'll come.

[*Exit Mrs Marsden. Anna stays behind to clear the tea things.*

JANE [*to Henrietta*]. Advertisement for what, I wonder. [*She snatches up a newspaper lying on the table and scans the front page.*] Ah, here it is—— (*Henrietta looks over Jane's shoulder and Jane reads*] "Wanted: Middle-aged lady of kind disposition, as Matron for country home for old ladies." [*She throws down the paper in disgust.*] Humph! More money being thrown away. [*She turns swiftly to Anna.*] Anna, you must have noticed Mother's strange behaviour lately?

ANNA [*leaving her work and turning to face Jane*]. Ye mean the master?

JANE. Yes, partly that. She talks as though he were still alive.

ANNA. And what's wrang wi' that, if it keeps her happy?

JANE. I believe you encourage her, Anna.

ANNA. I try tae understand. The mistress has explained it a' tae me, and I ken fine it's naething tae worry aboot.

JANE. But she can't go on living in that fool's paradise.

ANNA. Fool's paradise? Weel, there's worse paradises nor that. When auld age comes tae ye, Miss Jane, ye'll realize that the past is a sicht mair real tae ye than the present.

HENRIETTA. She may be living in the past, but she's spending in the present.

ANNA. Aye, and what aboot that? It's no' your money she's spending, is it? Ma mistress is happy in what she's daeing for others, and if she'll be poorer in one way she'll be richer in another. The Almighty looks after His ain.

JANE. That is enough of that, Anna. It is obvious that we shall get no help from you.

ANNA. Help forbye! Ye should be glad your mother found a way oot o' her grief. She's no' just day-dreaming i' fool's paradises, as ye seem tae think. Her ain suffering has made her think of others worse off than herself—puir auld bodies wi'oot a corner tae call their ain.

JANE. I was coming to that. Don't you see that her mind must be deranged? No sane person would speak of the dead as she does. And now this giving of her house to a lot of old women who will not appreciate it——

ANNA [*breaking in*]. And how dae ye ken what the auld appreciate? You've never done onything for them.

JANE. You forget yourself, Anna.

ANNA. Aye, and I'm no caring aboot that. I ken fine what ye're after—the twa o' ye.

[*Sweeping up her tray, Anna exit.*

HENRIETTA. What insolence! We shall have to stop this old-ladies'-home business, Jane, or we shall have Mother penniless on our hands.

JANE. Well, you wanted Mother with you, didn't you, Henrietta? You were at pains before we came to give me several good reasons why *you* should have Mother rather than I.

HENRIETTA. But naturally, Jane, I expected her to contribute to the household expenses. I am a poor woman, remember.

JANE [*snapping*]. Miserly, you mean. Your bank balance is big enough; that hotel of yours is a gold mine. I suppose you thought you could live on Mother if she made her home with you.

HENRIETTA. That is a wicked lie, Jane. You were very anxious to have Mother yourself until you realized she would be poor.

JANE. Arguing like this will get us nowhere; we must do something.

HENRIETTA. Yes, but what?

JANE. The only way to stop Mother's mad impulses is to have her put under control. The first step is to get a doctor to her.

HENRIETTA. Well, that is a useless suggestion. You know Mother would never consent to seeing a doctor.

JANE. I know, but I have an idea. Marian Lorne has come back to their old house across the road. She has been a doctor for years now. I ran into her yesterday. We could ask her to call, ostensibly to look Mother up, but really to keep her under observation.

HENRIETTA. Excellent idea! You can see her to-morrow, Jane, and explain.

JANE. No. We must take the opportunity now. I know Marian will be in because she asked me to call about this time—any day. Now if you telephone her when Mother is back in here, I'll see that you are not disturbed and that Mother is kept on the right—er—plane until Marian comes.

HENRIETTA. Oh, I'm not good at explanations, Jane. You do the telephoning; any little thing like that upsets my nerves so.

JANE [snapping]. Oh, never mind your nerves for once, Henrietta. Think of your bank balance! If I left Mother to you, you would have hysterics all over the place and ruin everything. Look! [Fishes in her handbag] Here is Marian's card with the telephone number. Go quickly, now; Mother's coming. Explain, of course, that we suspect Mother's mind is going.

HENRIETTA [as she goes out through the garden door]. Oh dear, I'm sure to say the wrong thing.

[Enter Mrs Marsden through house door.

MRS MARSDEN. What a dreadful woman! An ex-wardress who wants to be matron to my old ladies. She has a voice like a rasp and kept shouting things like "plenty of discipline" and "toeing the line," as though my poor old ladies were a bunch of criminals.

JANE. They probably are.

MRS MARSDEN [suddenly noticing the absence of Henrietta]. Where is Henrietta? That girl can't sit still for five minutes.

JANE. She's gone into the kitchen for some recipes she wanted.

MRS MARSDEN [jumping up]. Then she must come out of the kitchen. The last time Henrietta went recipe-hunting we missed a jar of ginger. I must go after her.

JANE [sharply]. No, Mother, it's all right. Anna will be there. Please sit down. I want to talk seriously to you. The fact is, I sent Henrietta out of the way. I cannot possibly discuss Father when she has hysterics every time we mention him.

MRS MARSDEN [*sitting down*]. Oh, and what do you want to discuss? Not, I hope, my old age, Jane. You put ten years on my life when you bring that up. I'm sick to death of this what's-to-be-done-about-Mother expression you've worn on your face ever since your father's death.

JANE. I think you are very ungrateful, Mother. [*Sighs.*] But I suppose I must make allowances. After all, you are going through a very difficult period. Once we have got over your difficulties——

MRS MARSDEN. Difficulties? Have I got any?

JANE. Oh, I know you make light of them, Mother. We admire your courage. But don't you think you would be happier in the long run if you gave way to your grief? Then you will be able to get away from Father.

MRS MARSDEN. Get away from Henry! My dear Jane, you do not understand. I should never get away from Henry, and, what's more, I don't want to get away from him. But please, let us not discuss it. If you can't understand, then just accept it as a little eccentricity of mine.

JANE. Now, Mother, I'm convinced that what you need is a long rest in a quiet, bracing spot. We'll find a nice comfortable home in the country for you. Edward and I will straighten out your affairs for you so that you can leave at once.

MRS MARSDEN. For heaven's sake, Jane, go home and manage your own affairs. I'm sick of your interference. I am not a prostrate widow; I am not a sick imbecile; and I have every intention of carrying out my own plans.

[*Henrietta enters. She stands rather uncertainly in the doorway. She looks pale and upset. Mrs Marsden remarks this.*] You are as white as a sheet, Henrietta. What is it?

HENRIETTA. I thought I saw something in the hall—a sort of figure.

M

[*There is a sound of a distinctly masculine cough in the hall. Henrietta draws back towards Jane. Someone knocks. All start and Henrietta shrieks. Jane goes to open the door, but Henrietta pulls her back.*]

No, Jane. It might be——

       [*Here the door slowly opens and Anna's head pops round.*

ANNA. It's that Henry, ma'am.

       [*At the word 'Henry,' Henrietta rushes, screaming, through garden door. Anna enters.*

MRS MARSDEN. She's mad to behave like this.

JANE [*impatiently*]. What Henry is this, Mother?

MRS MARSDEN [*as she goes towards door*]. So that was it, the mention of Henry. Go after her, Jane, and explain that it is only Mr Henry the plumber who has called and not the shade of her father.   [*Exit.*

       [*Anna goes to table and tidies it, removing paper, string, etc., from parcels. With a gesture of impatience, Jane goes after Henrietta. Doorbell rings.*

ANNA. I doot that'll be the minister; he aye calls when the hoose is in an uproar, puir man. [*She goes to answer bell and, catching sight of Henrietta's abandoned flowers, whisks them up and takes them out. Off-stage Henrietta screams and Jane admonishes her in a loud and angry voice. Anna quickly returns with a tall sensible-looking woman of Jane's age. This is Dr Lorne.*] The mistress will be in presently, Doctor; she's engaged for the minute.

       [*Another loud scream from above. Anna and the doctor exchange a look.*

DR LORNE. Is that Miss Marsden?

ANNA. Aye, she was hysterical as a wean, but as a woman she's proper daft. She's been seeing things ever since she came intae the hoose. I'll tell the mistress you are here, Doctor.

       [*Exit Anna. Another shriek from Henrietta. The doctor shakes her head as though the patient were already a foregone conclusion. Enter Mrs Marsden.*

MRS MARSDEN. Ah, Marian, my dear, you are early.

didn't think you would get through my old ladies before evening——

DR LORNE. But I haven't, Mrs Marsden—not yet. I can't get near their lungs till they've got out their life stories, poor dears!

MRS MARSDEN. I know; they love to talk, poor things; but I'm so glad you've come. Henrietta is behaving like a lunatic. [*Another scream.*] Hark at her!

DR LORNE. Yes, I expected a patient. Perhaps I had better go up at once as she may do herself harm.

MRS MARSDEN. But the silly girl has locked herself in; Jane is up there trying to get in. You say you *expected* a patient; I don't understand. Do sit down and explain, my dear.

[*They sit.*

DR LORNE. A few minutes ago I had a telephone message from Henrietta; I'm afraid she is really ill.

MRS MARSDEN. Good heavens! Then she must have felt the attack coming on——

DR LORNE. But you don't understand, Mrs Marsden. Henrietta telephoned me on *your* account—not hers.

MRS MARSDEN [*taken aback*]. On *my* account.

DR LORNE. Yes. Henrietta said that she and Jane had come to the conclusion that you were mentally deranged.

MRS MARSDEN. That I was mentally deranged? Good heavens! then the poor girl is mad. But wait. You said *Jane* and she had come to this conclusion?

DR LORNE. Ah, yes, but of course Jane would have nothing to do with such a mad statement; it is poor Henrietta's delusion that your mind is going.

MRS MARSDEN. Humph! I wonder. When they were little, Jane usually managed to make Henrietta the scapegoat. I think I understand. You know, Marian, I have a feeling that you will agree with me when I suggest that Henrietta be removed to some quiet, bracing spot for a nice long rest. Isn't that what you do to—er—border-line cases?

DR LORNE. Sometimes. It may be all that Henrietta needs. It may be only a temporary mental disturbance. Yes, a few weeks in a quiet, bracing spot is the idea; with the right people, of course.

MRS MARSDEN. The right people?

DR LORNE. Yes. A home for nervous cases. I know of a very good one run by an American Alienist.

MRS MARSDEN. Ah, American. Expensive, no doubt. Splendid! I mean we must spare no expense for poor Henrietta. The cost will be an essential part of the cure. She must never for a moment be allowed to feel that the expense is being considered. I must insist on that, Marian. After all, Henrietta can afford it and her health comes first. A few weeks of this er—luxury home should cure her for life.

[*Scream.*

DR LORNE. I sincerely hope so. We must do something about getting that door open.

MRS MARSDEN [*ringing for Anna*]. I'll have the plumber sent up. Perhaps he can force it. My dear, you'll scarcely believe it, but I started the afternoon quietly with a few roses and a cake; since then I have acquired a ghost masquerading as a plumber, and a demented daughter.

DR LORNE. A ghost?

MRS MARSDEN. Just one of Henrietta's. That is how all the screaming started. She got it into her head that Henry—her father—was haunting the house.

DR LORNE. Quite off her balance, poor soul. However, once we get her away——

MRS MARSDEN. Ah yes, once—we—get—her away!

[*Enter Anna.*

ANNA. Oh, ma'am, I couldna come before. We were trying to open the bedroom door when Miss Henrietta saw the plumber; she gie'd sic a scream and threw that photy of the master in 'is cricketing things right at poor Mr Henry. He's bleedin' a' doon his face, and Miss Jane has rushed him off tae the chemist. [*Turning to Dr Lorne*] I forgot i' the excitement that we had a doctor i' the hoose.

MRS MARSDEN. What next?

DR LORNE. We shall have to remove Henrietta; we can't have this violence. I'll go up to her now, but you stay here and relax, Mrs Marsden. Anna can go up with me.

MRS MARSDEN [*as Dr Lorne and Anna turn to go*]. Very well, Marian. Oh, Anna, that photograph—[*Anna turns back, but Dr Lorne goes out*]—I hope it isn't badly damaged.

ANNA [*bringing photograph from the top of her overall*]. Here it is, ma'am; it's no' hairmed. Just a wee bittie off the end of his moustache. [*They examine it together.*] Ye can get it touched up.

MRS MARSDEN [*taking photograph*]. You go up to the doctor, Anna. I'll wait for Miss Jane.

ANNA [*as she goes*]. Verra weel, ma'am.

[*Alone, Mrs Marsden gives a deep sigh, lies down on the divan and becomes absorbed in the photograph of Henry.*

MRS MARSDEN. Such a lot of little boy in you, Henry, my dear. You were out for a duck that day, I remember, but you looked so handsome in your white flannels. How I wish the house would be quiet!

[*Enter Jane. She looks hot and breathless, not to say untidy.*] Oh, it's only you, Jane. I quite expected to see Lady Macbeth or Alice in Wonderland. It's that sort of afternoon, isn't it?

JANE [*flopping down in a chair*]. I have a splitting head. But, thank heaven, Henrietta seems quieter.

MRS MARSDEN. Yes, she is being well looked after at the moment.

JANE [*wearily*]. I went for a doctor. You will remember Marian Lorne who used to live across the road. She's come back to their old house. However, she was out on a case, so I left a message that she should come over on her return.

MRS MARSDEN. How is the plumber, poor man?

JANE. Oh, you've heard about that. That man is going to

make trouble. I got the chemist to patch him up a bit, but he means to make you pay heavy compensation.

MRS MARSDEN. Indeed he deserves compensation, but I rather think Henrietta will pay that. Haven't you got a little confused, Jane? It was Henrietta, not I, who did violence to the plumber.

JANE. But you are the real culprit. You terrified Henrietta with your talk of Father. She simply isn't responsible at the moment.

MRS MARSDEN. Ah, if you want to go deeply into the matter of cause and effect, Jane, I might argue that if you and Henrietta had not given me a birthday present of a tombstone decoration, the plumber would now be peacefully mending the boiler pipes and claiming compensation from nobody.

JANE. Oh, you have an answer to everything. [*She gets up and walks about impatiently.*] Oh, why doesn't Marian come?

MRS MARSDEN. Oh, she's here. Didn't I tell you?

JANE. Marian *here*! Why didn't you tell me? Where is she?

MRS MARSDEN. She is attending Henrietta.

JANE [*starting to door*]. Then I must see her at once.

MRS MARSDEN. Just a minute, Jane.

[*Jane turns to her mother.*

JANE. What is this—a conspiracy? All this secrecy about Marian.

MRS MARSDEN. The conspiracy, my dear Jane, is entirely yours. I was expecting Marian in any case. She is helping me to choose twelve old ladies from fifty who have applied for flats.

JANE. So she is in league with you. She mentioned nothing of this to me yesterday.

MRS MARSDEN. I asked her to keep the whole thing to herself. By the way, Jane, Marian shares your enthusiasm for quiet, bracing spots—for *mental* cases, you know. Now, Jane,

I know I can depend on you to do your best for poor Henrietta. What a blessing she has you to manage her affairs!

JANE. Manage her affairs? What is this?

MRS MARSDEN. Well, my dear, surely it is obvious. Seeing that Henrietta has usurped my position as a candidate for a quiet, bracing spot, surely you will do for her what you were so willing to do for me.

JANE [*spluttering*]. Why—what—I——

MRS MARSDEN. I knew I could count on you. That is settled then. You can arrange Henrietta's affairs so that she can get away quickly for the rest she so badly needs.

JANE. That is rot, Mother. You know as well as I do that there is nothing seriously wrong with Henrietta. All she needs is a good slap.

MRS MARSDEN [*chuckling*]. She'll get that all right when the bill comes in. The bill, I understand, will be very heavy. Cost a lot to run, you know, these places.

JANE. But it's ridiculous!

MRS MARSDEN. Perhaps, but not nearly as ridiculous as it might have been.

JANE. I can make Marian understand. I shall explain.

MRS MARSDEN. I shouldn't try if I were you, Jane.

[*Enter Anna.*

ANNA [*Mrs Marsden sits up*]. It's the plumber, ma'am. He's that mad, ye canna see his face for sticking-plaster. He says he'll ha'e the law on Miss Henrietta. He asked to see you, but you look tired, ma'am. It's a shame—all this on your birthday. I'll tell him you'll see him to-morrow, shall I, ma'am?

MRS MARSDEN. But the poor man must be taken care of, Anna. Miss Jane will see to him. If it is plumbing, I'm always available to Mr Henry; but until he is well enough to get back to my pipes, Miss Jane will take care of him. She will see that he gets his rights, won't you, Jane?

JANE [*furious*]. Oh, this is too much, I'm going home.

[*She gets up and moves towards door.*

MRS MARSDEN. Then collect the plumber, Jane; otherwise I shall send him on!

[*Exit Jane, slamming the door. There is the sound of an angry male voice. A loud altercation goes on between Mr Henry and Jane in the hall. This is followed by a loud slam from the outside door, and then silence. Mrs Marsden smiles at all this. Anna gives a sigh of relief when the door slams.*

ANNA. Weel, that's yin oot, and the ither is practically in the madhoose. What a day! Me mither was recht when she said it was easier to rear half a dozen lads than one lass. I'm thinking, ma'am, [*she puts Mrs Marsden's feet on a cushion and arranges more at her back as she talks*] that the auld ladies will be a rest cure after your ain flesh and blood. Aye, cuckoo clocks an' a'. Ye can stop a clock, but no' yon twa.

[*Mrs Marsden laughs.*

MRS MARSDEN. I wonder what's going on upstairs, Anna.

[*At this moment Henrietta bursts in. She looks very wild and distraught. Dr Lorne, watching like a hawk, follows.*

HENRIETTA [*to Mrs Marsden*]. How dare you get a doctor to me?

MRS MARSDEN. I did not get a doctor to you, Henrietta. You sent for the doctor yourself. It's the one sensible thing you have done this afternoon. All that screaming—locking yourself in a room—assaulting a harmless plumber!

HENRIETTA. I was upset. I thought I saw Father.

MRS MARSDEN [*to Dr Lorne*]. There, Marian! You see, the poor girl suffers from hallucinations too; her father has been dead for nearly a year. I think you are right about that home. Better six weeks now than a complete breakdown later on.

HENRIETTA. Home—breakdown! There's nothing wrong with me—or there won't be once I get out of this madhouse.

DR LORNE [*gently but firmly pushing Henrietta down into her seat*]. There, my dear, don't worry; just keep quiet and relax.

HENRIETTA [*shrilly*]. Quiet? I'm quiet enough; it's the rest of you who are mad.

ANNA [*pityingly*]. Aye, that's what they do say, puir things.

MRS MARSDEN. My poor Henrietta. I'm afraid it is a choice between a rest in the country or hard labour in gaol.

HENRIETTA. Gaol? I——

MRS MARSDEN. I'm afraid so. The plumber is the mildest little man when he's plumbing, but not when he has been smashed on the head with a photograph frame; he threatens proceedings.

HENRIETTA [*on a high note*]. But it was an accident. I lost my head.

MRS MARSDEN. Exactly, my dear, and you can find it in the country. It's so peaceful, isn't it, Marian? Where is your home?

DR LORNE. Miles from anywhere and as silent as the grave.

MRS MARSDEN. And dirt cheap—a mere hundred pounds to regain one's health and sanity.

HENRIETTA [*hoarsely*]. A hundred pounds!

[*She half faints. Dr Lorne supports her.*

DR LORNE. Don't worry, Mrs Marsden. I'll take her across to the surgery and I think I had better keep her with me for the night. I want to keep her under observation.

[*She helps the hysterical Henrietta to the garden door.*

ANNA. Will I help ye, doctor?

DR LORNE. No, I'll manage. You see that Mrs Marsden has no more excitement.

[*Dr Lorne and Henrietta go. Anna closes the door after them and Mrs Marsden lies back on her settee. As Anna turns—*

MRS MARSDEN. Well, Anna, I think we shall have peace now. Miss Jane will be nicely occupied with the plumber and Henrietta will have her work cut out convincing Dr Lorne that there is no patient.

ANNA. Aye, as I said before, they had the wrang soo by the lug. Noo, the rest o' this birthday ye'll ha'e tae yoursel'. Put up your feet noo— [*she puts Mrs Marsden's feet on the settee and arranges cushions at her back.*] I'll awa' and mak ye a nice cup o' tea.

> [*As an afterthought, Anna puts the roses nearer the settee. She goes to the door and looks back as one might on a favourite child. She goes out. Alone, Mrs Marsden fingers the roses and smiles tenderly at Henry.*

MRS MARSDEN. I expect it was the gardener, Henry, but I like to think it was you; your lovely roses, my dear.

CURTAIN

THE PHANTOM SHIP

by Mary F. Matheson

CHARACTERS

MRS HATTIE HOOPER, 55, *widow* — Eunica
LUCY HOOPER, 22, *her daughter* — Ann
MARY LOU BANKS, 42, *spinster* — Marie
GRACE MERRILL, 26, *American tourist spending night at house* — Jackie

SCENE: Living-room of cottage in village on coast of Nova Scotia

TIME: Late August evening

THE PHANTOM SHIP

C.R. is an entrance from rest of house. Cornered R. back is large fireplace, open hearth, with kettle swung from iron bar across opening. To R. front of fireplace is large rocker, on L. stool. Back, near L., is door to kitchen. Couch, cabinet for dishes, chairs, lamp, centre table, hanging shelves, and corner shelves for ornaments provide other furniture. Spinning wheel or frame with hooked rug in process would give atmosphere. Completed hooked rugs may be hung on wall. Furniture should be simple, i.e., home-made chairs, etc., painted. Coloured cushions give comfortable appearance. C.L. is a window, deep set, curtained.

Mrs Hooper, Lucy, and Mary Lou have soft voices.

At opening of curtain the stage is in fire-light. Grace Merrill is sitting at table C., making notes in small book, and humming softly to herself. Mrs Hooper is sitting at window, working on rag rug. Grace makes her last memo, closes book, and turns to Mrs Hooper.

GRACE. So there's to be a wedding here to-morrow.

HATTIE [*putting away her work, as it is getting too dark to see*]. Yes, my daughter's. My only child.

GRACE. Won't I be in the way to-night? You must be busy.

HATTIE. No! We Nova Scotians prepare ahead. Lucy's things have long been ready. You'll be no trouble.

GRACE. Good!

HATTIE [*starting to lay the table, in which Grace assists, offering to take cutlery from Mrs Hooper*]. As long as you don't mind supper being late.

GRACE. Not at all. Tea refreshed me.

HATTIE. We'll have it in about an hour. Clif will be here then.

GRACE. Is Clif the lucky man?

HATTIE. Yes. He drove over to see his mother to-day!

GRACE. His last day of single blessedness with his mother, eh?

HATTIE. She's an invalid, poor soul.

GRACE. I suppose your daughter is with him?

HATTIE. No. She felt this was his mother's day. Lucy will be in any minute.

GRACE. I hope she won't think me a nuisance.

HATTIE. She won't.

GRACE. It's my lucky day. A good seven hours behind the wheel through the loveliest country—to find a haven like this!

HATTIE. I'm glad you like it.

GRACE. I love it. The simplicity of everything. The village so peaceful, this cottage, then—[*sinking into seat at window*] this lovely sunset.

HATTIE. It's a pity you can't stay longer.

GRACE. I'm sorry too. I must get that Boston boat to-morrow. Next week—the classroom again!

HATTIE [*going towards kitchen*]. Holidays soon fly!

GRACE. Yes, but I'll come another year!

[*Exit Hattie. There is a pause. Mary Lou enters C.R. carrying a cloak and unlighted candle. She is dressed in long dress of soft blue—a dress about 20 years old. She places cloak on chair and turns to window with candle, but stands motionless as Grace (looking through window) blocks her way. Grace senses presence and turns—surprised and nervous when she sees Mary Lou. Finally she manages to speak.*]

You—wanted—Mrs Hooper?

MARY LOU [*pointing at window*]. The window!

[*Grace hurriedly rises and steps free of window. Mary Lou advances and tries to light her candle, but is unsuccessful. She turns back towards room. Grace is watching her fascinatedly and questioningly. Mary Lou shakes her head.*]

[*Enter, and stand in kitchen doorway, Mrs Hooper.*]

No matches!

> [*Mary Lou glides from the room, carrying the candle.*

HATTIE [*weakly*]. Oh! That's quite a shock!

GRACE. I'm sorry. Can I help in any way?

HATTIE. No, thank you.

GRACE. Perhaps you would like to be alone?

HATTIE. No. Don't go. It's very foolish of me. It's seeing Mary Lou in that dress.

GRACE. It means something?

HATTIE. Yes, it means something all right.

GRACE. Can't you tell me?

HATTIE. It's so long since she has worn it—I thought it was leaving us in peace!

GRACE. Leaving you in peace?

HATTIE. When she wears it, it means one thing only—*The Phantom Ship!*

GRACE. *The Phantom Ship?*

HATTIE. She must have seen it to-day!

GRACE. Isn't there something I can do?

HATTIE. Yes; would you mind going to Mrs Jeffrey—just next door? Ask her if she has seen the ship to-day.

GRACE. Of course, but I didn't see a sign of one as I drove along.

HATTIE. Oh, no, my dear, you couldn't see it!

GRACE. Why not?

HATTIE. It is only seen by those who have lost someone at sea.

GRACE. Good heavens!

HATTIE. Yes.

GRACE [*unbelievingly*]. Now, Mrs Hooper——

HATTIE. That's why! [*Pause.*

GRACE. Then Mrs Jeffrey has lost someone?

HATTIE. Yes.

GRACE. And she—the girl in the blue dress—has she lost someone?

HATTIE. She too!

GRACE. How terrible!

HATTIE. Whenever it comes to the Bay she is usually the first to see it! It is only then she wears her blue dress.

GRACE. But why?

HATTIE [*opening door to kitchen*]. I'll tell you later. Would you mind going to Mrs Jeffrey now—before *she* comes back?

GRACE. All right.

> [*Exit Grace L.B. Hattie is perturbed. Mary Lou again glides into room, this time carrying a lighted candle.*

HATTIE. Mary Lou!

> [*Mary Lou smiles very gently and happily.*]

The candle to-night?

MARY LOU [*with quiet excitement*]. It has come again!

HATTIE [*switching on light*]. Are you sure? It's been so long since you saw it!

MARY LOU [*happily*]. It's come back at last! [*Placing candle in window*] This is to show George the way to me.

HATTIE. I see. You have dressed?

MARY LOU. I didn't want to keep George waiting.

HATTIE. Of course not! So pretty!

MARY LOU. Do I look nice?

HATTIE. Oh, yes. It's a very lovely dress; but, Mary Lou, you've had it such a long time. Don't you think you would like to wear your new one—for George?

> [*Mary Lou is bewildered.*

MARY LOU. My new one?

HATTIE. You know—the pretty grey one I've just made you—for Lucy's wedding to-morrow!

MARY LOU. Oh, no. This is George's dress. I must wear this one.

HATTIE [*pleadingly*]. Just to please me!

MARY LOU. I can't.

HATTIE. Do, Mary Lou! It's newer and fresher!

MARY LOU. No! This is George's dress!

HATTIE. Oh, Mary Lou, for Lucy's sake I want you to wear the other dress. Won't you change?

MARY LOU [*shaking her head*]. NO!

HATTIE. You must understand. I don't want a shadow on the house to-night. I want happiness!

MARY LOU. But I'm happy and I won't cast a shadow on the house. I am going down to my gulls!

[*Mary Lou picks up cloak.*

HATTIE. No. You mustn't go out!

MARY LOU. Just till the ship comes into dock.

[*Enter Grace.*

HATTIE. Oh, Miss Merrill, this is Miss Mary Lou.

GRACE. How do you do?

MARY LOU. I am well, thank you.

HATTIE. Miss Merrill is staying with us overnight.

MARY LOU [*to Grace*]. Do you like my dress?

GRACE. It is pretty!

MARY LOU. It is my wedding dress.

GRACE. I see.

MARY LOU. I am going to the Bay. My gulls are there!

[*Exit Mary Lou, smiling, and taking cloak.*

HATTIE. Don't mind anything she says to-night!

GRACE. I understand.

HATTIE. You saw Mrs Jeffrey?

GRACE. Yes.

HATTIE. Has she seen it?

GRACE. Yes. She says she saw it in the sunset!

HATTIE. It is here, then! [*Walking to and fro*] I don't know what to do for the best, but I must keep this from Lucy to-night!

GRACE. Why should you?

HATTIE. I didn't want to tell you—— There is going to be a tragedy—a sea tragedy!

GRACE. No one can know that beforehand!

HATTIE. Oh, yes. Those who can see the ship!

GRACE. Those who can see the ship?

HATTIE. The ship—it is a sign of sorrow!

GRACE. Oh!

HATTIE. My daughter will be in soon, but I can't wait. Don't tell her it has been seen.

GRACE. But won't she see it before she comes in?

HATTIE. No.

GRACE. She hasn't lost anyone?

HATTIE. She was too young when her father and uncle were drowned.

GRACE. I understand!

HATTIE. I must go after Mary Lou. She has gone down to the rocks, but I'm always afraid she might not stop at the rocks.

GRACE. You go ahead. I won't tell your Lucy.

HATTIE. Thank you. Clif will soon be here too. Lucy will be all right then.

GRACE. I'll wait for her!

HATTIE [*turning to go, stops*]. Here she is, I think!

[*Enter Lucy, dressed in summer clothes.*

LUCY [*kissing her mother*]. Hello, Mother!

HATTIE. Glad you're back, Lucy! Had a good time?

LUCY [*throwing coat and hat on chair near window*]. Lovely!

HATTIE. Miss Merrill, this is my daughter. Lucy, Miss Merrill is staying the night!

GRACE. How do you do?

LUCY [*shaking hands with Grace*]. Very well, thank you. I'm glad to welcome you!

HATTIE. Lucy, Mary Lou and I are going for a walk.

LUCY [*seeing table set*]. But it's so near supper.

HATTIE. Mary Lou has gone. I must go after her. You go right ahead with supper—it's all ready.

LUCY. I couldn't eat a thing—I'm too excited.

HATTIE. You may be, but you'll have to think of Miss Merrill. It isn't her wedding eve.

N

LUCY. I'm sorry. Of course, I'll get supper.

HATTIE. I'll hurry!   [*With an anxious glance at Grace.*

GRACE. Don't worry about us!

[*Mrs Hooper, thus encouraged, smiles as she leaves room.
Lucy goes to mirror.*

It has been a funny sort of day, hasn't it?

LUCY. Very—so bright in the morning, the squall, then so lovely and clear again.

GRACE. The fog is beginning to come over now! ✗

LUCY. Yes, it changes quickly. I hope all the bad weather came to-day.

GRACE. You don't want rain to-morrow, eh?

LUCY. I should hope not!

GRACE. It does spoil things.

LUCY. It's unlucky too!

GRACE. You don't believe that?

LUCY. Not believe it?

GRACE. Surely not! It's only superstition.

LUCY. Maybe, but——

GRACE. It's just an old-fashioned idea.

LUCY. Perhaps, but we're a superstitious people!

GRACE. Not you, though?

LUCY [*slowly*]. I'm afraid I am—a little. Sometimes I've tried to tell Mother I'm not, but—deep down—I know I am.

GRACE. I can understand it in the older folks, but didn't believe it of the younger ones.

LUCY. It's bred in us. The life here. Everything!

GRACE. I guess it's a hard life!

LUCY. For some—very!

GRACE. Yours?

LUCY. Mine has been happy!

GRACE. Lots of pleasant memories, eh?

LUCY. Yes! A few of the other kind too!

GRACE. I guess few escape them.

LUCY. I suppose so. One of the first things I remember

was when I was very, very small. I was in my bed. It was Mummie's too. I wakened with someone sobbing—quiet—quiet. It was Mummie. I put out my hand in the dark. I got her face. It was so wet—even her hair was wet. I tried to stroke her cheek—and she gathered me into her arms as if it were I who needed the comforting. That was when Daddy went away.

GRACE. When you were very small?

LUCY. Yes, I was only two.

GRACE. Poor child!

LUCY. Not "poor child"! It was "poor Mummie"! I was all right. She was mother and father to me.

GRACE. Yes!

LUCY. Funny—I seem to remember very clearly things that happened long ago in the night!

GRACE. I guess that is because your first memory was of something in the darkness.

LUCY. I don't know. But after that, so often, I can remember seeing Mother in the candlelight—we didn't have electricity in those days—bending over the other bed in our room. Sometimes it was almost light and she would still be wearing her day clothes! The other bed was Mary Lou's. Have you seen her?

GRACE. Yes, I met her.

LUCY. Poor Mary Lou. She was sick then. She has never been quite right since.

GRACE. She is one of your mother's relatives?

LUCY. Not really, although I look on her as a sort of aunty. She was to have married Mummie's brother, but he was lost at sea with Daddy. She's lived with us ever since.

GRACE. Three to feed and clothe!

LUCY. Yes. Mother had to work hard!

GRACE. Sewing, I suppose?

LUCY. Sewing, boarders, rugs, quilts—anything!

GRACE. I've seen some of her work. It is lovely!

LUCY. It's part of the life here—for the women!

GRACE. And for the men—the sea?

LUCY. Yes—the sea! Mostly!

GRACE. Just at seasons, of course.

LUCY. Oh, all the year round, practically. They follow the catch. Here for cod at one time, some place else for herring, and at another time and place, halibut—and so all round the coast.

GRACE. What a life! For the women at home, and the men at sea!

LUCY. It's cruel!

GRACE. Yet the men must go out. It gives them their living.

LUCY. It gives, and it takes!

GRACE. I suppose it does!

LUCY. It has taken its toll out of every home in the village. It's greedy! It's—it's never satisfied! That's why I'm glad I'm marrying a land man.

GRACE. I guess I don't blame you.

LUCY. It robbed me—I never knew of just how much. It steals here, there, and yonder, piling up debts and responsibilities. Someone has to pay!

GRACE. But the women—they must be prepared for it!

LUCY. Some hope, some dread—some are resigned, I think —but IT is impartial!

GRACE [reflectively]. No wonder you're marrying a land man!

LUCY. I'd never have a sea-going one. I would hate his master!

GRACE. The sea?

LUCY. Yes, the sea!

GRACE. I might too—if I knew it like you. But I love it. I love to watch it—love to see the sun's sparkle on it—to see a storm dip into it—to see the moon send a pathway over it— even love it shrouded in mist.

LUCY. Oh, at times, I don't really hate it, but I'd rather have a windswept hillside and security—the security of a man's protection for my children and myself—all the time!

GRACE. I would want that too!

LUCY. Maybe I'm a coward. Maybe I'm not made of the stuff my mother is—but I couldn't be both father and mother to my children!

GRACE. One never knows—until tried! But you won't have to be! You are about to have all your wishes fulfilled!

LUCY [after a pause]. I'd better see about supper. Clif will soon be here!

[Lucy goes towards window to get her coat. In doing so she catches sight of candle.]

Oh!

GRACE. Anything wrong?

LUCY. No. Oh, no!

GRACE. I thought you'd got a fright!

LUCY [pointing to candle]. No. Do you know why—that is there?

GRACE. The candle?

LUCY. Yes, the candle.

GRACE. No. Isn't it usually there?

LUCY. It is not!

GRACE. I think it is a nice idea. I've read so many stories—old-fashioned ones, you know—where a light in a window has guided someone to safety.

LUCY. Do you know who put it there?

GRACE. No——

LUCY. You said you saw Mary Lou?

GRACE. Yes.

LUCY. What was she wearing?

GRACE. What was she wearing?

LUCY. Yes—what colour was her dress?

GRACE [hesitatingly]. I—I—don't know. She was wearing a cloak. She went out ahead of your mother.

[Lucy lifts candle, deliberates.

LUCY. It's a long time since it was in this window!

[*Lucy finally carries it over to mantel.*

GRACE. Why do that?

LUCY. I don't like it there!

GRACE. But what difference can it make?

LUCY. We don't need a light in the window!

GRACE. There's nothing wrong, is there?

LUCY. No. There couldn't be. Nothing to affect me, anyway.

GRACE. That's good. You made me feel queer!

LUCY. Sorry!

GRACE. I wouldn't let a little thing like a candle worry me!

LUCY. Of course not. It was just a flash through my mind.

GRACE. Let's forget about it, then!

LUCY. Surely! Here they're back!

[*Lucy stands facing door, anxiously waiting.*

HATTIE [*entering*]. We weren't long!

LUCY. Mother?

HATTIE. Yes?

LUCY [*fearfully*]. Mother!

HATTIE. What is it, child?

LUCY. Is everything all right?

HATTIE. Of course, dear. What do you think would be wrong?

LUCY. I don't know. Mary Lou?

HATTIE. She's all right.

LUCY. I was afraid! [*Lucy hears Mary Lou in hall. She peers through door.*] I must see her! [*When she does see Mary Lou in hall-way*] OH!

HATTIE [*in pity*]. Lucy!

LUCY [*after pause*]. I was right. She's wearing the dress!

HATTIE. Yes!

LUCY. She has seen the ship?

HATTIE. I imagine she has!

GRACE. You were going to tell me why she wears it when she has seen the ship.

HATTIE. The first time she saw it, she lost George. She believes he went away on it.

GRACE. Yes?

HATTIE. Each time it appears she expects he will return to her, and she is waiting—ready to marry him!

GRACE. Oh!

HATTIE [*pleadingly*]. Lucy, don't let it worry you.

LUCY. Don't let it worry me! I know too well what it means!

HATTIE. Don't think about it!

LUCY [*defiantly*]. No. No, of course not. Why should I? It can't touch me anyway. You're here. Mary Lou is here, and Clif must be on his last few miles.

HATTIE. Then he'll be here too! So cheer up!

[*Embracing Lucy.*

LUCY. Yes, of course!

HATTIE. Well, let's forget about it—and be happy to-night!

LUCY. You've been down to the Bay, Mother?

HATTIE. Yes.

LUCY. Any sign of a storm?

HATTIE. No. It's quiet, with some fog.

LUCY. Are there any boats out?

HATTIE. None but the ferry. The others are all tied up.

LUCY. I'm glad. I feel better! [*Breaking from mother's embrace*] And yet——

HATTIE. Don't think anything more about it. Think of to-morrow.

LUCY. I am. That's why I'm unhappy. It will spoil to-morrow!

HATTIE. Perhaps not!

LUCY. Oh, yes. It will!

HATTIE. Maybe not! It may be for someone away along the coast!

LUCY. You know when it's seen here, it's for someone in the village. Someone will be sad to-morrow. Someone will not be able to come to the wedding. And Clif will feel it badly.

HATTIE. Yes, Clif will!

LUCY. Oh, why, after waiting so long, had it to come at this time?

GRACE. Don't borrow trouble! You were happy a few minutes ago, weren't you?

LUCY. Yes.

GRACE. Then why let a dress, a candle, a ship—chase it away?

LUCY. It's what they mean.

GRACE. It's just superstition. What you fear may never come!

LUCY. You don't know it!

GRACE. Of course I don't, but no matter what you think——

LUCY. You don't understand. We know. Whenever it comes it brings grief—all around. Those who have already suffered see it and are sad. Each time it comes someone new sees it, and within the round of the clock that person hears of the loss of a loved one!

GRACE. That may be coincidence!

LUCY. Coincidence! It's easy for you to speak. You come and play by the sea for a month or so. We have to live with it—live with it—and die with it! We know it—what it sends to us—and what it takes away! Oh, Mother, why should it send to-night—why? Why? [*Lucy breaks into sobs.*

HATTIE. Lucy! Lucy!

GRACE. I'm sorry for you. Sorry for you all to have such a fear over you—but—look here—you're losing control!

HATTIE. Yes, my dear, pull yourself together!

GRACE. Come, now, what if your young man came in and found you like this?

HATTIE. Yes, Lucy, think of Clif!

LUCY. I'll be all right. Don't worry!

[*Lucy becomes more composed.*

GRACE. That's better!

LUCY. Sorry. I've been foolish.

GRACE. I guess you are a little tired!

LUCY. No. I'm all right! Mother, have you seen it?

HATTIE. I haven't looked!

LUCY. Oh, you haven't looked?

HATTIE. No.

LUCY [*deliberately*]. You've been afraid to look!

HATTIE. Not afraid! If I'm meant to see it—I will!

[*Mary Lou glides in. She is carrying cloak. She places it on one of the chairs.*

MARY LOU. My candle! Who has taken away the light—George's light?

LUCY. I put it on the mantel!

MARY LOU. But I have seen the ship!

LUCY. When?

MARY LOU. This afternoon. I was down feeding my gulls. They seemed so restless to-day. Kept flying over the Bay, then back they would come to me!

LUCY. I know the way they go—so noisy!

MARY LOU. But to-day they weren't crying! There was a stillness. The air was soft. The wind was gentle. The tide was at its height. The waves broke gently on the rocks and fell back upon themselves, for all the crannies were already full. I began to feel very strange—almost afraid.

HATTIE. Oh, Mary Lou—I'm sorry I wasn't with you!

MARY LOU. Then a shadow came. I looked at the sun. It was going behind a cloud. As I looked, long streamers came down from the sun to the Bay.

LUCY. They say the sun is drawing——

MARY LOU. Oh, it doesn't matter what they say. But just where the rays struck the water—away out—there was the ship!

LUCY. Oh!

MARY LOU. It was so lovely. I was happy again—so happy!

HATTIE. I'm glad you are. It never comes without bringing grief!

MARY LOU. I don't understand how it can do that!

[*Mary Lou has gone to the window.*]
The fog hides it now!

[*Lucy is at table disconsolate. Her mother tries to comfort her. She smiles very faintly.*]
Lucy, wasn't it lovely!

HATTIE. Lucy can't see it!

LUCY. No. I've never been able to see it. Won't be able to see it now.

HATTIE. Of course not!

MARY LOU. Oh, look—people, lots of them—running down to the Bay.

HATTIE. People going to the Bay?

MARY LOU. Yes.

HATTIE. How do you know? You can't see through the fog?

MARY LOU. I see their lanterns bobbing along.

HATTIE. Let me see!

[*Hattie goes to window and stays there for the following, peering out between speeches.*]
Yes, there's quite a crowd!

LUCY. I wonder why?

HATTIE. I don't know.

MARY LOU. The ship must have come in. Oh, why didn't we stay longer? Why did you bring me back?

HATTIE. What can be happening?

MARY LOU. We should have waited. Oh, I can't see the ship now!

[*Lucy draws near window and would like to look out, but fears to do so.*

HATTIE [*suddenly*]. The ship? It's right there—under the bank of fog!

LUCY. Oh, Mother! You see it?

HATTIE. The crowd. There is someone leaving it now. Coming this way.

LUCY. Can you tell who it is?

HATTIE. No! I can just see the lantern. He is hurrying!

LUCY. It may be Clif. Let me see, Mother!

HATTIE [*making room in window beside Mary Lou and self*]. Of course, child.

LUCY. Where is he?

HATTIE [*pointing*]. There! Near our gateway now!

LUCY. I see the lantern.

MARY LOU [*suddenly, pointing out over Bay*]. Look, there! There it is! All lit up now!

[*Lucy and Hattie unconsciously do as bidden and look. Hattie sees ship. She looks at Lucy. Lucy, too, has seen ship—gives smothered gasp, in fear, a clenched fist to chin.*

LUCY. Mother! Mother! I see it! I see the ship!

HATTIE [*murmuring consolingly*]. Lucy! Lucy!

LUCY. It's for me—this time!

[*Meanwhile Mary Lou is oblivious to others. She is listening to unheard voices. Suddenly she leaves the window.*

MARY LOU. He's calling me. I'm coming. George, I'm coming!

[*Mary Lou dashes from room—L. back.*
[*There is a knock at door—C.R.*

LUCY. Mother, he's dead. Somehow, Clif is drowned!

[*Hattie goes out C.R. Lucy and Grace await tensely her return.*
[*There is a mumbled message—the words "Clif," "Accident," "Bay" being heard.*

HATTIE [*off-stage*]. Thank you!

[*Lucy has collapsed at table, C.*
[*Enter Hattie.*

HATTIE. He was late, and took the ferry. Little Billy Yates fell into the Bay. Clif saved him, but was drowned himself.
[Lucy, in the silence that follows, slowly recovers, then very quietly.

LUCY. Mary Lou, Mother. *[Pause.*

HATTIE. Will you be all right?

LUCY. Yes. You go to Mary Lou. *[Exit Hattie.*
[Lucy goes to mantel, takes candle, smiles gently at Grace—as Mary Lou has smiled all evening—walks to window and places candle on sill—then turning to Grace]

To guide them home!
[Lucy picks up Mary Lou's cloak, puts it round her shoulders, smiles dazedly and glides off. Grace makes an involuntary movement to stop her, but refrains, and aghast with sorrow and sympathy she drops into chair at C. table.

CURTAIN

TWO WOMEN

by Eileen Russell and Herbert Chown

CHARACTERS

MRS MILLER
MRS BRETT

TWO WOMEN

The scene is the bedroom of a small cottage.

Mrs Miller, a woman of about 65, is sitting in an arm-chair (high-backed) with a pillow behind her, a shawl round her shoulders, and an eiderdown over her knees. She is knitting, slowly and deliberately. She has been ill but has the full use of her hands (and intelligence). Beside her is a small table on which is an oil lamp alight, some medicine bottles, including one smallish, black one marked 'Poison,' medicine glass, etc.

It is about 4 P.M. on a winter's afternoon. A certain amount of light comes from the window, but as the play proceeds the room perceptibly darkens except for the circle of light thrown by the lamp.

There is a wireless set somewhere in the room. It is turned on. The music is cheerless.

The bedroom door is open. There is the sound of a knock on an outside door.

MRS MILLER. Come in.
> [*The bedroom door is pushed wider and Mrs Brett comes in. She is a handsome, purposeful young woman of 28 to 30. She is of the working class, but considers herself superior to Mrs Miller. She is rather made-up, her hair waved, etc. She does not like Mrs Miller and is rather apprehensive as to why the old woman has asked her to come. Therefore she is from the first rather too bright and chatty to be natural and is quick to take offence. Her speech is common-refined, Mrs Miller's that of an old country woman. Mrs Brett (Irene) is carrying some flowers—cheap, yellow chrysanthemums.*]

Oh, it's you at last, Irene. Come in and shut the door.

MRS BRETT. How are you, Mrs Miller? It was nice of you to ask me to come. I brought these for you.

MRS MILLER. Not out of your own garden, I'll be bound.

MRS BRETT. No. As a matter of fact I bought them. They looked so bright.

MRS MILLER. Turn that thing off, do. I can't hear myself speak. Mrs Wood left it on when she gave me my dinner. It gets on your nerves, that noise.

MRS BRETT [*turning off the wireless*]. I like a bit of music myself, but I do like it to be cheerful. It's a nice set.

MRS MILLER [*watching her closely as she mentions Tom, her son*]. Tom made it. He understands them things.

MRS BRETT [*very brightly and casually*]. Well, what I always say is if you can understand the inside of a motor-car you can understand anything.

MRS MILLER. Tom's clever.

MRS BRETT. I'm sure he is.

MRS MILLER. About them sort of things.

MRS BRETT. And doing so well in his job, too—so I hear.

MRS MILLER. They don't find no cause for complaint at the garage.

MRS BRETT. Shall I put these in water?

MRS MILLER. There's a vase over there. [*Grudgingly*] They're pretty.

MRS BRETT [*bringing the vase to the table near Mrs Miller and arranging the flowers in it*]. You need something pretty with all these ugly medicine bottles about.

MRS MILLER. They don't do me no good. Doctor says I'm to try this and that—outside and in. But nothing does any good. Waste of money, that's all it is.

MRS BRETT. I shouldn't think poison would do much for you.

MRS MILLER. That's for me eyes. I suffer something cruel with me eyes. But poison on the label or no, it's all the same. They put that on to make you pay more.

MRS BRETT. But you're ever so much better, aren't you?

MRS MILLER. Who says I'm better?

MRS BRETT. Well, you wouldn't be allowed to have visitors if you weren't.

MRS MILLER. You can call it better if you like—tied hand and foot and likely to be.

MRS BRETT. It's a shame. And you used to be so active.

MRS MILLER. I'm old now.

MRS BRETT. You'll soon get strong again.

MRS MILLER. No, I shan't. I shan't never be no different to this. I'd better make up my mind to it. But when a woman can't look after her home—and her son—she'd better be dead, to my thinking.

MRS BRETT. It's no use getting morbid. Tom's all right, I'm sure. And glad to do what he can for you. And so are the neighbours. We all are.

MRS MILLER [with a sudden unpleasant look at her]. What have you done for me, Irene?

MRS BRETT [very bright to hide fear and awkwardness]. Oh, me? Well—I didn't see what I could do. I never was much good at nursing. Besides, I didn't like to come till I was asked.

MRS MILLER. So you thought I should ask you.

MRS BRETT. Well . . . no, I didn't—not really. I was ever so surprised.

MRS MILLER. And did you wonder why I asked you?

MRS BRETT [more and more worried; trying to hide it]. Well, I thought you wanted a bit of company.

MRS MILLER. There's a good many comes in for a word with me.

MRS BRETT. Of course there is. They know you need cheering up.

MRS MILLER [grimly]. They tell me the news.

MRS BRETT [increasingly apprehensive]. I never think there is any news in this place.

MRS MILLER [watching closely]. There's always something going on in the village.

MRS BRETT. Nothing really worth talking about. It's a dead-and-alive hole. I always said so.

MRS MILLER. Funny you chose to come back and live in such a hole after you was married.

MRS BRETT. Oh well, with Jack away at sea I wanted to be where I knew people. It was only natural.

MRS MILLER. Maybe. How is Jack?

MRS BRETT [*happier, thinking she is on safer ground*]. Oh, he's all right, or he was when he wrote last. It takes a month of Sundays for letters to get here. I reckon he's having a gay time all right.

MRS MILLER. It's not every one thinks about gay times. China, isn't it?

MRS BRETT. Yes. I told him he'd be chasing bandits. He's seen the world, Jack has.

MRS MILLER. Naval men has no busi....

MRS BRETT [*frightened* ....not.

MRS MILLER. A ....

his wife.

MRS BRETT. C ....

days.

MRS MILLER [....

MRS BRETT. ....

MRS MILLER. ....

MRS BRETT. I ....

MRS MILLER. ....

MRS BRETT. ....

I don't know ....

MRS MILLER ....

know what's ....

MRS BRETT ....

What's goin ....

of. I suppo ....

about me.

MRS MI ....

o ....

and I've got me brains and I can use them even if I am tied here.

MRS BRETT. What do you mean? You can't know anything about me. There isn't anything . . .

MRS MILLER [*shooting it at her*]. You're going with my Tom.

MRS BRETT [*acting righteous indignation for all she is worth*]. Going with Tom—me? That's likely, isn't it? Tom—of all people. That's a wicked lie.

MRS MILLER. It's the truth.

MRS BRETT. It's not. It's downright wicked to say such things.

MRS MILLER. It's not me that's wicked.

MRS BRETT. You are—if you believe such things. Why, Tom's only a boy—twenty-two, isn't it? If I wanted a man—which I do n' ___ ___ I'd choose a boy years younger th ___

___ be a fool.

___ ink such a thing

___ ath knowing it.
___ Tom? He may
___ isn't me.

___ You've got

___ to be talked

___ ed to the door.
___ ack.] Come
___ ruth, Irene.

___ It is a con—

___ s. Why

shouldn't we? It was nice of him to ask me, seeing I was all alone, with Jack miles away. But I ought to have known what people would think in this place.

MRS MILLER. He went home with you . . .

MRS BRETT. Of course he saw me home.

MRS MILLER. He went indoors with you.

MRS BRETT. I had a drop of beer in the house. I couldn't do less than ask him to have some.

MRS MILLER. He came home at four in the morning.

MRS BRETT. I can't help what time he came home.

MRS MILLER. He told me he'd been sent out from the garage to bring people back from a dance and they'd broken down. Lies . . . You've taught my son to tell me lies.

MRS BRETT. I can't help what he tells you.

MRS MILLER. Took you in to the town to a dance last week, didn't he? To a dance for every one to see . . .

MRS BRETT. For an hour or two. And no one with any decency would see any harm in that. Tom always did have a fancy for dancing with me.

MRS MILLER. And you had a fancy for something more than dancing. You got hold of Tom. He was a decent lad. I've brought him up decent. There's never been anyone could gossip about us. And then you come along with your painted face and your shameful clothes, got up like the strumpet you are . . .

MRS BRETT [*half crying with rage*]. You—you insolent old woman. I'll tell Tom what you've been saying about me.

MRS MILLER [*slowly*]. You won't tell Tom anything, my girl. You aren't going to see Tom again.

MRS BRETT. Oh, aren't I?

MRS MILLER. You're not going out of this room until you've given me your Bible oath you'll not see him again.

MRS BRETT [*defiant*]. We'll see about that.

[*She takes a cheap cigarette case out of her bag and lights a cigarette.*

MRS MILLER [*changing her tactics, her eye on Irene all the time to watch her reactions*]. Think, Irene, think. You can't have changed so much from when you was a little thing. So pretty and good you was then—pretty as a picture and quite the lady. You was the same age as my Bert what died, and almost as delicate as him then. But we all thought you'd do well for yourself if you lived to grow up. And sure enough you did, with your education and your work in the town—no going out to service for you. And you married well and everybody respected you. We got used to thinking you was a cut above us, Irene. And now you're just letting yourself down. You, a married woman, going about with a boy like Tom.

MRS BRETT [*sullen now*]. It's my own business what I do.

MRS MILLER. It's your business if you ruin yourself. But it's my business if you ruin Tom.

MRS BRETT. I'm not doing Tom any harm. He's as well with me as with any of the village girls.

MRS MILLER [*shrill*]. No harm . . . To be talked about the way people are talking about you . . . To spend money the way he's been spending it on you.

[*It has slipped out but it is the most heartfelt part of her determination to rescue Tom from Irene.*

MRS BRETT [*seizing the point*]. Is that what you've been worrying about? The money. . . . The paltry few shillings Tom has been spending on me . . .

MRS MILLER. Few shillings . . . He hasn't brought home not more than half his wages this month and more. Said he had to buy a new suit—or tyres for his bike . . .

MRS BRETT. You can't expect a grown man to hand over his money like a little boy.

MRS MILLER. And I should like to know why not? It's all I've got . . . except the pension. Tom's all I've got. Who else is to keep me, if not Tom?

MRS BRETT [*insolent, trying to get her own back*]. I see. Is that

what you're worrying about? That Tom might find someone else to spend his money on. I never thought of that.
It's all right, Mrs Miller. I won't be too much an expense
to him. I'll see that he pays the rent and buys you your
medicines . . .

MRS MILLER. You won't see to nothing. I won't have Tom
running after you . . .

MRS BRETT. Spending his wages on me, you mean.

MRS MILLER. You're shameless, that's what you are.

MRS BRETT [*stubs out cigarette*]. You need not talk like that
any more. The money is all you care about. I understand
now.

MRS MILLER. You're not going to see Tom again. Do you
understand that?

MRS BRETT. You can't separate me and Tom, and it's no
good your trying.

MRS MILLER. I can and I will, my girl. You'll find that
out.

MRS BRETT. You can't. You can screech at him the way
you have at me. He won't care. You can set the neighbours
on to talk. He won't care about that either. I tell you he
loves me.

MRS MILLER. And what will Jack Brett have to say when he
hears that? Even in China you can hear news of home.

MRS BRETT [*the idea of Mrs Miller's writing to her husband is a
new thought to Mrs Brett. She has to bluff*]. Jack knows.

MRS MILLER. What?

MRS BRETT [*confident now because the bluff has succeeded*]. Of
course he knows. I told him. I told him I'd met someone I
cared for more than I could ever care for him. [*Quoting reck-
lessly from the films as she improvises*] I told him I'd found the
real thing at last. And he said he'd arrange for a divorce and
then I shall marry Tom.

MRS MILLER [*her turn to panic now*]. That you won't . . .

MRS BRETT. I'm afraid I shall.

MRS MILLER [*with an instant change of tactics to tearfulness*]. You can't. You can't do it.

MRS BRETT. And why not?

MRS MILLER. Tom's all I've got.

MRS BRETT. You can't expect to keep him for ever. He's got his own life to live and so have I.

MRS MILLER. And you think you're going to live it with him—eh?

MRS BRETT. Yes.

MRS MILLER [*tearful*]. It's hard, when you get old and you've only one son left, to have him leave you.

MRS BRETT [*with a proprietary air which maddens Mrs Miller*]. Tom won't forget you. He'll do the best he can.

MRS MILLER [*searching her mind for what she can do*]. And I must do the best I can.

[*Her restless glance falls on the bottled marked 'Poison.'*]

MRS BRETT [*with a sigh of relief*]. That's right. That's the way to look at it. [*A little anxious*] Tom will be back soon, won't he?

MRS MILLER [*absent-mindedly*]. Half-past five.

MRS BRETT [*more happily*]. Oh, not till then? I can't stop so long.

MRS MILLER [*as if half to herself*]. Marriage—eh? Who'd have thought you meant to get married? We wasn't like that in my day. Once married always married it was then. None of this chopping and changing. There was children too. They gave us plenty to think of. Nowdays you reckon you're clever—but you're not clever enough. Children keeps a woman busy till she's too old to want anything but peace. You ought to have had children, Irene.

MRS BRETT. Nonsense. I'm too delicate.

MRS MILLER. Do you think Tom won't want children?

MRS BRETT. He won't want me to suffer. [*Really frightened by the suggestion*] I might die.

MRS MILLER. There's plenty do. [*Taking pleasure in Irene's fright*] But we didn't stop to think about that. You're a coward, Irene, a coward—that's what you are.

MRS BRETT [*defiantly*]. Do you think it's cowardly to face up to what everyone's saying about me and Tom?

MRS MILLER [*grimly*]. That's not courage. In my day we'd have known what to call it—sin.

MRS BRETT. You don't understand. Everything is different now.

MRS MILLER. There's some things can never be altered. "Thou shalt not commit adultery . . ." It's in the Book. You can't alter what's in the Book.

MRS BRETT [*in her superior tone*]. You can't alter two people that love one another.

MRS MILLER. So you think Tom loves you?

MRS BRETT. Think it . . .? I know it.

MRS MILLER. There's a truer name for it in the Book. Many's the time I've thought of the day when Tom would bring a girl home and tell me she was the one he'd chosen. But I never thought it would be like this.

MRS BRETT. Well, I didn't want you to hear it like this. It was you that started it. The way you went for me. People should mind their own business.

MRS MILLER. When my son breaks the Commandments it is my business—twenty-two years old or no. But it seems I was too late. What's done is done, and what's broken is past mending.   [*Cries a little.*

MRS BRETT. It'll all be forgotten in a little while. You'll see. We shall all settle down quite happy.

MRS MILLER. Tom's father would have beaten the life out of him. But what's a mother to do.

[*Another glance at the bottle.*

MRS BRETT. Let him alone to look after himself, I should think.

MRS MILLER. Maybe. It's hard being old and being a woman. And losing the use of your legs so you can't do nothing day after day but sit and think from morning till night . . . from the time the light comes until it goes again. [*Noticing how dark it is getting*] It's getting late now. [*Querulously*] I could fancy a cup of tea, but I can't get it till Tom comes in.

MRS BRETT. I'll get it for you.

MRS MILLER. That would be good of you, Irene. Get one for yourself too. You'll find the kettle on the gas ring. It should be near the boil and the tea-things will be put ready. Get yourself another cup and pour it out down there. There's nothing so heartening as a cup of tea and I need heartening. You'll understand in time how an old woman feels.

MRS BRETT. Well, we all have to get old, don't we? So perhaps I shall.   [*She goes out.*

[*Mrs Miller clears a space for her tea-things on the table beside her. Again she sees the medicine bottle. She picks it up to move it. Then stays with it in her hand, thinking. The ideas that have been coming and going in her mind now crystallize into determination. With a most unpleasant smile she takes the cork out of the bottle and carefully pours its contents into the vase of flowers. She replaces the cork and puts the bottle ready to her hand.*

[*Mrs Brett comes back with two cups of tea.*

MRS MILLER [*eagerly*]. That's right. Put it down here, Irene.

MRS BRETT [*with a return to her first bright manner*]. Looks better than the medicines, doesn't it? If it was me I couldn't bear to have all these bottles about—especially this one. [*Almost touching the dark bottle*] Shall I move it over there?

MRS MILLER [*shrilly*]. You leave my bottles alone. [*Recovering her composure*] I can't get about to fetch nothing when I need it. Give me my tea here. I'm wanting it. Tom will be back before long, but I never wait for him if I can get someone to fetch it in for me.

MRS BRETT. I can do with a cup any time myself.

MRS MILLER. And you're going to have one now. Just draw

the curtains first, will you? And pull down the blinds. [*Mrs Brett goes to do it. Mrs Miller watches her.*] Be careful, now. It sticks. That's right. That's nice and cosy. Now come and have your tea.

MRS BRETT [*taking the cup*]. Thanks. Did I make it strong enough?

MRS MILLER. Oh yes, it's strong enough. There's something left for me while I can still enjoy my tea.

MRS BRETT. It'll do you good. There's nothing like it when you're feeling a bit down. Makes you feel better at once, doesn't it?

MRS MILLER. Yes, it makes me feel better. [*She watches closely until Mrs Brett has drunk the last drop. Then suddenly she leans forward and almost shouts at her*] But it won't make you feel better, my girl. You think you'll marry Tom, do you? You won't give him up, won't you? You will. You'll be giving him up any minute now. Do you see this—the poison it would scare you to have about? I put it in your tea, Irene. In your tea . . .

MRS BRETT [*screams*]. What . . .? [*Gasps and puts her hands to her throat, then partly recovers herself.*] No . . . no . . . You couldn't do that . . . It's not true . . . You couldn't . . . I don't believe it . . .

MRS MILLER. Don't you? But you will. I'll show you. Look . . . [*She holds up the bottle.*] Look at this . . . The bottle was full . . . Look at it now . . . It's empty . . . I put it in the tea . . . all of it . . . in your tea . . .

MRS BRETT. But . . . but it will kill me. It'll . . .

[*Starts to choke.*

MRS MILLER. Yes, it'll kill you . . . It is killing you now.

MRS BRETT [*screaming now*]. Help me . . .! Oh, my God . . .! Help me . . .! I . . .

MRS MILLER. Afraid of dying, are you? That's the way of all cowards. But the wages of sin is death. . . . It's in the Book . . . Death.

MRS BRETT. You wicked, wicked woman . . . You'll hang for this . . .   [*She staggers and falls.*

MRS MILLER [*calling gently, as if to see if Irene is conscious or not*]. Irene . . . Irene . . .

    [*There is no reply. Irene lies still. Mrs Miller smiles grimly to herself and takes up her knitting.*

CURTAIN